Praise for Yasmin Boland

'Yasmin Boland is a pioneering voice in modern astrology. This book and her Moonology™ Oracle Cards *are known the world over and have become beloved tools for anyone working with the Moon for healing and guidance. When someone tells me they want to learn astrology, I often reply, "You need Yasmin Boland."'*

Kyle Gray, bestselling author of *Angels Are with You Now* and *Raise Your Vibration*

'Yasmin Boland is a masterful astrologer whose grasp of the celestial influences on the human soul is unsurpassed.'

Sonia Choquette, *New York Times* bestselling author of *Trust Your Vibes*

'Yasmin Boland has a gift for making all things Moon and astrology make sense! Yasmin is here to translate the messages of the stars and the Moon and she has a special way of making astrology simple.'

Rebecca Campbell, bestselling author of *Light Is the New Black* and *Rise Sister Rise*

'Yasmin Boland is probably the greatest living astrological authority on the Moon. Buy this book... Yasmin knows her stuff.'

Jonathan Cainer, the late, great astrologer

'Yasmin Boland is one of the most gifted astrologers of our time. Her Moonology teachings have guided millions back to their intuition, rhythm and personal power, including me. Her work is very clear, soulful and life-changing. If you want to understand the Moon, manifest with it and truly transform your inner world to create magic, Yasmin is the guide you can trust.'

Sarah Prout, author of *Dear Universe 365*

'Being in tune with the Moon's natural 29-day cycle as it waxes and wanes can have a dramatic impact on your life, helping you achieve what you really want.'

Daily Express

Moonology™

WORKING WITH THE MAGIC OF LUNAR CYCLES

YASMIN BOLAND

HAY HOUSE
Carlsbad, California • New York City
London • Sydney • New Delhi

Published in Australia by:
Hay House Australia Publishing Pty Ltd, www.hayhouse.com.au
P.O. Box 7201, Alexandria NSW 2015

Interior illustrations: shutterstock

A catalogue record for this book is available from the British Library.

Tradepaper ISBN: 9798318604225
E-book ISBN: 978-1-83782-755-8
Audiobook ISBN: 978-1-83782-753-4

Printed in Australia by McPherson's Printing Group

This product uses responsibly sourced papers, including recycled materials and materials from other controlled sources.

The authorized representative in the EU for product safety and compliance is Penguin Random House Ireland, Morrison Chambers, 32 Nassau Street, Dublin D02 YH68, Ireland. https://eu-contact.penguin.ie

For Olivier and Louis –
I love you to the Moon and beyond!

The secret of making something work in your life is, first of all, the deep desire to make it work: then the faith and belief that it can work: then to hold that clear definite vision in your consciousness and see it working out step by step, without one thought of doubt or disbelief.

Eileen Caddy, founder of Findhorn

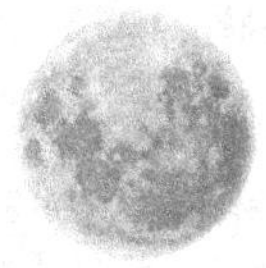

Contents

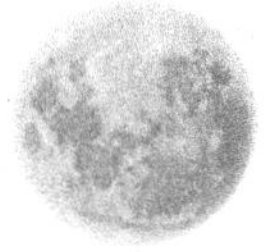

Introduction

The Moon is earth's oldest temple holding the
potency of countless prayers since the dawn of time...
a bell whose ringing brings you into the field of the
Mother, where body and *soul can* quietly drink.

DANA GERHARDT, *MOONCIRCLES*

Would you believe me if I told you that the Moon can be used as a fantastically simple cosmic timer to help you create the life you dream of?

Well, it can. How do I know? Because it's worked for me and for hundreds, or even thousands, of my readers over the past 20 years that I've been writing about manifesting with the Moon on my website, yasminboland.com. And now, as you read about and start to use the practices and information contained in this book, it will work for you too: you can become a powerful Moon manifester.

To use the Moon as a tool to create the life you want, you simply need to become aware of the lunar cycles and understand the basic principles of manifesting. This book will show you how to do both of those things.

If you've dabbled in manifesting but have found that so far not much has materialized, the information in this book may well be the missing link you need. It shows you how to work with the lunar energies to supercharge your wishes and dreams.

Manifesting with the Moon's cycles as a cosmic timer dramatically boosts our chances of becoming accomplished conscious creators and deliberate manifesters.

You don't need to be an astrologer to do this either. In fact, you don't even need to believe in astrology. Nor do you need to know any maths, or astronomy. It's really easy to work with the Moon without knowing too much about the whys and wherefores. The Moon is up there nearly every night for us to see. We're connected to Her and She's connected to our planet. That's all you need to know as a starting point.

The secret is to make wishes and set intentions in tune with the Moon's cycles. Over the years I've received hundreds of emails from people letting me know about their success in manifesting their goals, thanks to their regular use of New Moon wishing. And that success is what I'm hoping to pass on to you within this book.

You'll learn about how and why New Moon wishes work (they really do) and how the Full Moon dovetails with and aids and abets that process. (In fact, the work you do on yourself at the time of the Full Moon will be what stands you in good stead for manifesting your dreams at the time of the New Moon two weeks later.)

You'll also learn how to make the most of each New and Full Moon depending on which sign of the zodiac they're in. And you'll discover how to deduce the part of your personal horoscope chart that each New and Full Moon is affecting. This information can then be used to predict what you can expect in the weeks afterwards.

How the book works

I've organized the book into four parts.

Part I is an introduction to connecting with the Moon, and includes an overview of the nine main Moon phases. By understanding these phases, each of which has a certain rhythm, and the key things to do during each one, you'll learn to dance to the Moon's rhythm and find that life flows more easily – it will be as if you've cracked a secret code. I also explain the neuroscience behind Moonology – how every New Moon intention, Full Moon release and Dark Moon surrender seemingly align with how our minds rewire themselves through focus, action and letting go.

Part II is all about the New Moon and New Moon wishing – how to do it and why it works. I explain why this is a practice you should perform every four weeks for the rest of your days!

It also means knowing which sign of the zodiac the New Moon is in. Armed with this information, you can start to work with the themes and energies of each lunation. It's a powerful process and you don't need to know any astrology in order to do it.

Also in the New Moon section, I guide you through how to work out very quickly and easily where the monthly New Moon is taking place for you *in your personal horoscope chart*. Each month the New Moon triggers a part of your astrological chart called a House, and I show you what you can expect as a result.

You'll also learn how to use the New Moon to improve your life by connecting with the Archangels and Goddesses, discover the best time to tackle certain tasks and work with powerful affirmations, and much more. The idea is that you can create, plan and predict your life using the New Moon as a timer.

Part III focuses on the Full Moon. As well as being beautiful and sending down numinous moonbeams, the Full Moon speaks of heightened emotions, tugs-of-war in our lives, climaxes and the opportunity to release negativity. In this section I show you how best to use the energy of the monthly Full Moon as She moves through each zodiac sign. We also take a look at the power of Full Moon forgiveness and gratitude, and the way these in turn power your New Moon wishes.

Plus, you'll see how the sign the Full Moon is in can be used to support any efforts you're making to live consciously and in tune with the Universe. You'll also see how to work out in which part of your own chart the Full Moon is taking place from one month to another, and what that means for you.

Part IV looks at how to live consciously with the Moon. You'll discover what the Daily Moon means for you and begin to understand how to connect with Her energy each and every day. I invite you to step into the folklore of the Moon and explore how centuries-old names, such as the Wolf Moon and the Harvest Moon, grew from humanity's timeless urge to mark life by nature's rhythm, not the clock. You'll also learn about the sacred power of ritual – where fire, water, air and earth unite with the Moon's rhythm to help you anchor your dreams in the real world.

Along the way I introduce you to the eclipses, which occur in accordance with the New and Full Moon. When an eclipse hits your chart strongly, it can be life-changing (trust me: I've seen it for myself)!

All this means that within one year, you'll have worked on pretty much every aspect of your life needing attention.

I've tried to present everything in the simplest way possible. To make things even easier, where appropriate, I've included links to pages on my website where you can find further information or download worksheets.

So climb aboard, we're off to the Moon!

PART I

Why the Moon Is Magic

What many deliberate manifesters don't realize is that starting the manifesting process at the time of the New Moon dramatically boosts our chances of achieving our dreams.

CHAPTER 1

Get in Tune with the Moon!

Let me begin by telling you my favourite New Moon wishing story. To do that, I need to rewind to when I was a 13- or 14-year-old girl growing up in the city of Hobart in the Australian state of Tasmania. In case you haven't heard of it, Tasmania is an island at the bottom of the world, to the south of mainland Australia. The only thing that stands between it and Antarctica is a whole lot of *very* choppy water and icy air Trust me, I know: I've sailed it!

Wishing on a dream

Back then, my main dream was to get out of Tassie and go live in Paris, France. I put pictures of Paris on my bedroom walls; I read French poetry and I listened to French music. The first dish I ever learned to cook was Quiche Lorraine because, well, because it was French! At one point I even managed to get my hands on a pack of Gauloises cigarettes – not to smoke them, but to burn them like incense in my room as I imagined I was a chic Parisienne sitting in a dimly lit Latin Quarter café listening to jazz. (Unfortunately, my mother smelled them, thought the worst and I was in a lot of trouble.)

Fast-forward to many years later. I'd qualified as a journalist and was staying in Paris for a week because a friend had offered me the keys to his flat while he holidayed in Australia. It wasn't my first trip to my dream city – far from it – but it was the first time I'd visited it as an adult, and my first time there alone.

As it happened, I arrived in Paris on the night of the New Moon. So, naturally, I headed straight for the Eiffel Tower to make my New Moon wishes. I figured that the tall spire would be a perfect conductor to send my wishes into the heavens. And that proved to be the case.

My wishes that day reflected the fact that I wanted to stay on in Paris for much longer than the week I was booked for. I was a single freelance writer – which meant I could work pretty much anywhere with my laptop, as long as I had an internet connection – and I had the right passport. Now that I was in Paris, with all these things in my favour, *why on Earth would I leave?* After making my wishes, I made my way back to my friend's flat. As I walked through the beautiful Paris streets at dusk, a voice inside my head said very clearly: 'Right: I live here now!'

'*Ha!*' I thought, '*What a strange thing for me to think!*' And yet, that's exactly what happened. The following day, I spotted a handwritten sign advertising an apartment to rent in one of the most chic districts in Paris, close to where I was staying. I went to meet the charming owner (who I later discovered was a European princess) and she showed me the flat. It was perfect; the only 'snag' was that the owner's husband had a photography darkroom off the kitchen, which the couple wanted access to from time to time. For this reason, the rent was *half* what it would normally have been in this amazing part of town, just off the Boulevard St Michel.

To make things even easier, the owner and her husband spoke perfect English, so I was able to communicate fully with them (my university French still needed some work). They offered me the apartment, and of course I said '*Oui!*' straight away. And so it was that I ended up living in Paris for the next two and a half years.

So, did just *wishing* to live in Paris make it so? Well, not exactly. Rather, I had the *dream* of living there, and then I *did something* about it (studying French and visiting Paris). Plus, I totally crystalized my dreams by making my wishes under the Eiffel Tower. The point I'm making is that we're always manifesting. We can't help it. Dreaming (worrying) of messing up your life? Then you may well do that. Dreaming of living in Paris? Then you may well do that. My dreams of Paris created my reality.

A couple of hours after I'd signed the contract on my apartment, a stranger I met in a café told me: '*Vous avez faites un miracle*!' – 'You've made a miracle!' Apparently, it's not usually that easy for a foreigner to cruise into Paris and find a place to rent, let alone something affordable in the smartest part of town.

For me, it happened totally seamlessly: almost as if I'd wished it into existence. I was living my dream, and it just felt natural... and when things feel natural is when the magic can happen.

The Moon: key facts

Before we go any further, here are some key astrological facts that it's useful to know, in order to put all that follows into perspective:

1. The Moon takes about 30 days to orbit the Earth and travel through all 12 signs of the zodiac, spending just over two days in each sign.

2. There's a New Moon and then a Full Moon every two weeks. So the New Moon happens, followed two weeks later by the Full Moon, then two weeks later by the New Moon, and so on.

3. Astrologers use the word 'lunation' to talk about a New Moon or a Full Moon. So for example, we might say that the next 'lunation' is the Full Moon in Aries.

4. The Moon triggers the planets as She goes around the zodiac, and is thus a great astrological timer.

5. Your Moon sign describes your emotional style and what you need to feel safe, supported and connected.

But far more importantly for our purposes, here is a quick list of what the Moon is associated with, astrologically speaking: feelings, emotions, mothers, parenting, memories, femininity, the Goddess, witches, women, childhood, cycles, nourishment, heritage, habits, sensitivity, moods, fluctuations, subconscious, receptivity, domestic life, the public, feeding, nurturing, home, needs, and more.

The benefits of connecting with the Moon

As you become familiar with the practices featured in this book, I think you'll quickly see how powerful it is to connect with the Moon – by making wishes at the time of the New Moon, and releasing and forgiving at the time of the Full Moon (more on both of these processes later). You'll also see how amazing it is to work with the sign of the zodiac that the New and Full Moons take place in, and the insights that come from knowing where a New or Full Moon is affecting your personal horoscope. After a while, you'll probably start to count down the days to the next lunation.

If you're on the spiritual path (and the fact you're reading this book means you almost certainly are), connecting with the Moon will be pure magic. For one thing, the Moon itself is a reminder that there's more to life than the goings-on of our daily lives. I mean, just look at it! The Moon is a seemingly luminous floating thing out there in the sky. Even with the naked eye She looks amazing. (If you've never seen the Moon through a telescope, I'd highly recommend it. *It's awesome in the true sense of the word.*)

Watching the Moon from month to month and year to year will put you in touch with Her cycles and rhythms – it will help you to remember that we're all a part of something much bigger; that we're kids of the Universe. We're stardust. We're *so much more* than people who struggle to get to work on public transport and once there, compete with others for promotions.

We're makers of magic on a journey towards enlightenment. We're at one with the skies and the heavens and all that lies beyond, and even if we can't observe the heavens fully, or even give too much time to contemplating nature, connecting with the Moon reconnects us with the Divine – with our Divine selves and with the cosmos.

When you start to get in tune with the Moon's cycles, you start to connect with the cosmos and nature. We 21st-century humans tend to be quite disconnected from the latter. Of course, we don't all live in cities and spend hours a day in an artificially lit room, perhaps in front of a computer. But oh so many of us do, right? Getting outdoors and engaging with nature by watching the mysterious Moon is a real remedy.

You can watch the Moon from your local park or from your garden. If you don't have a garden, try your driveway. And if you don't have a garden or a driveway, you can watch Her from the street or from your window. I remember the first time I had a chance to watch the Moon building to full, night after night after night. I was in Thailand, staying in a beach hut. The skies were black and the Moon was a spectacle.

These days, when the Moon is nearly full, I love to have a good 'Moonbath' by just sitting under the brightness and soaking up the moonbeams. I do this with my son, too, to introduce him to the magic of the Moon. For the record, the night of the month when the Moon is fullest is a great time to cleanse your jewellery of any negativity: just leave it out (somewhere safe).

Connecting with the Moon is a great routine discipline to get into. By making wishes at the time of the New Moon, you'll start to manifest your dreams. That fact alone means you may come to believe, as I do, that there's something very powerful about the

New Moon. And as for the Full Moon, which is the time when we let things go, well, that's just common sense, isn't it? We need to release control of anything and everything – from toxicity to negativity – and we need to do it on a regular basis.

CHAPTER 2

Transform Your Life with the Moon Phases

For me, the most important aspect of connecting with the Moon is becoming aware of where in the lunar cycle She is at any time of the month. So let's start working with the Moon in the most general way possible – by following Her through Her nine *phases*. This information could quite possibly change your life!

You almost certainly already know the names of at least two of the nine phases – the Full Moon and the New Moon. And now read on...

The lunar month

Although the Moon appears to change shape in the sky as She moves through these phases – from New to Waxing, to Quarter to Full Moon, and back again – in fact, it's Her position in relation to the Sun and the Earth that's changing.

Here's a bit of technical stuff... Think of it like this: the Moon orbits the Earth, and the Earth orbits the Sun, and the Moon phases are a result of the changing angles between the Earth, Moon and Sun, as this takes place. The angles between the Moon and the Sun as the Moon orbits the Earth cause different amounts of the Moon to be 'lit up' from our vantage point here on Earth. This is why sometimes we see the whole face of the Moon lit up (the Full Moon) and at other times the Moon resembles a 'Half Moon' (the Quarter Moon).

Many, *many* Moons ago, humans noticed the repeating light-play of the lunar cycle, and gave each phase a different name. We also studied the energies that the different phases brought to bear on us, and enshrined that wisdom in astrology.

The illustration below shows how the phases change over the course of the Moon's 29½-day cycle. (Note that the angles shown are those created when we trace a line from the Earth to the Sun and from the Earth to the Moon. So 0° is the New Moon and once the Moon has moved 180° around the Earth, that's the Full Moon).

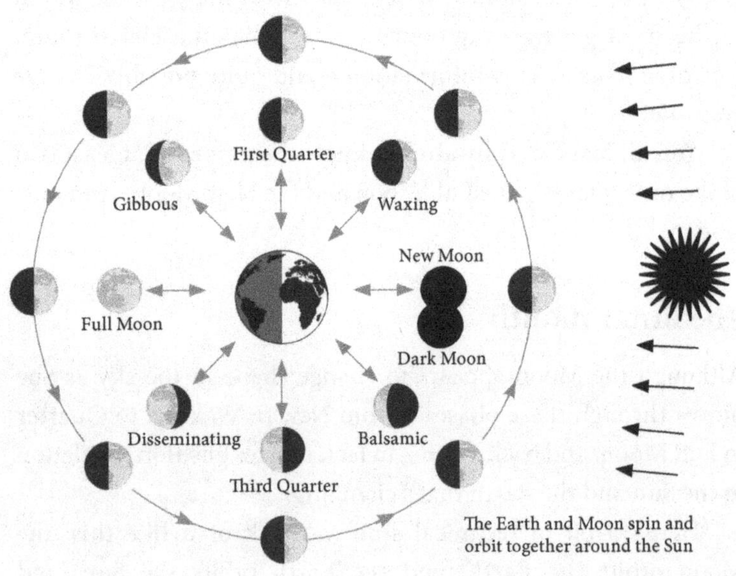

The nine Moon phases

It's also useful to know the following:

- A waxing Moon is moving from New to Full and getting bigger and bigger in the sky.
- A waning Moon is moving from Full back to New and getting smaller every night.
- We can think of the Moon in terms of the Chinese philosophical concept of yin-yang. The New Moon is a very yin time, but as the days that follow it unfold, it becomes more and more yang. The Full Moon is a very yang moment but as the days pass, the energies become more and more yin. (Isn't it beautiful, the way the Moon is in a constant state of flux, as we are, in life?)

A guide to using the Moon phases

For hundreds of years, tradition and folklore have declared that each Moon phase is 'good' for performing certain activities. And in 1967, American writer Dane Rudhyar published a seminal book called *The Lunation Cycle*, in which he explored the idea that the relationship of the Sun and the Moon in our birth chart is a big key to understanding our personality. It's a great book that all hardcore Moon manifesters should read.

Over the years, I've developed my own take on using the energies of each Moon phase – i.e. determining what we should and shouldn't do at each one, particularly in terms of manifesting our dreams – which I've outlined in the following guide. My approach is based partly on Rudhyar's work, plus common and traditional wisdom and my own experience.

Ideally, we'd all work with the Moon as She goes through all Her phases. However, most people will only think about which phase the Moon is in when they're having trouble in life – for example, if they've hit a rough spot and want some cosmic help.

And that's totally fine. The main thing is to understand that each Moon phase is good for one thing or another. Remember: the more you're in tune with the Moon, the more easily life will flow.

You can find out which phase the Moon is in by visiting my site, yasminboland.com. It's shown there every day on the home page. If you'd like this information sent directly to your inbox, sign up for my newsletters at moonologybook.com/dailymessage.

The New Moon phase

- Plant the seeds of your future dreams.
- This phase begins 1–3½ days after the Balsamic Moon.
- Keywords of this phase: *a clean slate, potential, dreams*

This is arguably the most exciting part of the lunar cycle. It might feel like a quiet time, when things are brewing, but in fact it's when you start to manifest your dreams – *or not.* This is a time to look forward to; to plan for; to make time for. Creation takes time. Reciting the mantra 'I am blessed' at this point in the lunar cycle will really help you.

At the time of the New Moon, ideas are coming from the ether and we must decide which of them we want to latch on to. We need to remember that anything is possible. This is definitely the time to think about what you *do* want, and not think about what you *don't* want. Meditate on your dreams. That will allow you to tune in to your higher self, so you have all the guidance you need to move towards them.

Having a massage is highly recommended at this time, or some hot sex, or even a hot bath – anything that reminds you that you're alive in your body. What are you planning to make of your experience as a human being?

If you're serious about being a deliberate manifester, the New Moon phase is when you should make time for yourself and put your wishes in writing or in a drawing. Writing works very well for most people; however, I personally think drawing or even doodling is even better. The reason for this is, creating a little drawing of your dream/wish means you're actually *visualizing* it coming true – and that's huge. It means you really start to believe it and when you do that, you start to manifest it. As they say, 'If you can believe it, you can achieve it.' (More about all this in Part II.)

Worried you can't draw? It doesn't matter. However, if you choose just to write down your goals, be sure to imagine them in your mind's eye as you do so. Feel them. To quote Dr Wayne Dyer: 'Feel the feeling of the wish fulfilled.' Feel it in your body. Feel the elation. Reading your wishes out loud is also very powerful. You'll radically accelerate your manifesting if you get this part of the cycle right (*see Part II for more on this*).

The Waxing Moon phase

- Explore your dreams.
- This phase begins 3½–7 days after the New Moon.
- Keywords of this phase: *courage, moving forwards, faith*

This is the time to allow your dreams to blossom and flourish. If it doesn't sound too poetic, think of yourself and your dreams as a flower that's opening up. Remember, the Moon is moving from being invisible to full power, and it's the same for your dreams. Right now you might not be able to see what you're going to manifest, but before too long they'll start to show up, just as the sliver of the Waxing Moon is showing up in the skies.

Keep thinking about what you want. Take a moment to go back to the wish lists you made at the time of the New Moon (more about this in Part II). Read them out loud. Think about them. Visualize them. Are they starting to feel real? If not, then read them again, and visualize them again. Feel the feeling of the wish fulfilled. Making wishes and setting intentions is a powerful beginning. If you really want to transform your life, then you need to stay with the vision.

The Waxing Moon is a time to keep the faith and to have courage. If you want something, you have to chase it. Sometimes it does take guts to go after what you want. Doing so can ignite a fear of failure. If you know this is an issue you struggle with, then you need to work extra hard at the time of the Waxing Moon not to give up before you've really got started.

The First Quarter Moon phase

- It's time to commit.
- This phase begins 7–10½ days after the New Moon.
- Keywords of this phase: *challenges, confidence, commitment*

This is when the Moon looks like a 'Half Moon' on the way from New to Full. At this point in the cycle, you may start to have a few doubts about your ability to manifest your dreams. Perhaps your resolve and/or commitment are being tested? If you know in your heart that you're no longer so wild about, or committed to, your old wishes, do yourself a favour and let go of them.

The ego might cling but you can let it go. If you're still feeling hyped about whatever you're working on, this is the time to double-commit to your dreams. Sometimes we need a hiccup to remind us that we're serious about something. This is a really important time to go back and re-read the wish lists you made at the time of the New Moon. Re-feel them. Re-visualize them. Re-imagine them.

It's also a time when some kind of crisis or issue could come up for you – all the better for you to work a little harder on your dreams. The astrological reason behind what's going on at this time is that the Moon is now just far enough away to clash with the Sun, making a hard angle. The angle, called a square, is known for creating an itch that needs to be scratched! In other words, issues that come up now call for some kind of action to be taken.

The Gibbous Moon phase

- Stay on course.
- This phase begins 10½–15 days after the New Moon.
- Keywords of this phase: *tweak, hone, adjust*

As the Moon gets closer and closer to fullness, it's time for stamina. Don't give up. Don't allow your ego, or fear, to spoil your plans. Stay open to whatever life is teaching you. If you know you need to make some changes to achieve your goals, make them now. Gibbous means 'bulging', and that very nicely describes the phase of the Moon when hopefully, life feels bulging with potential!

This is a great time to review your plans. There's a good chance that they could use some kind of tweak now. Spend some time going over your ideas and see what feels as though it's working and what feels like it might be about to run out of steam. This is the right time to build some kind of momentum, no matter what you're planning. But what if you've only just now come up with your plans? No problem. This is actually quite a good time to start new plans too.

It's important not to become impatient during this cycle. As the ancient Chinese philosopher Lao Tzu said: 'People in their handlings of affairs often fail when they're about to succeed. If one remains as careful at the end as he was at the beginning, there will be no failure.'

This phase is also good for getting back into any good habits or routines that you've let slip. We might be nearly two weeks away from the New Moon but ultimately, we're still in the building phase of the Moon cycle so restarting something now is still recommended.

The Full Moon phase

- It's make-or-break time!
- This phase begins 15–18½ days after the New Moon.
- Keywords of this phase: *results, forgiveness, gratitude*

The Full Moon is the high point of the lunar cycle. Things come to a head now, and we know it instinctively. If one of your wishes is to come true, it may well manifest at this point in the cycle. Or perhaps you'll simply get a strong sign that it's on its way. Some wishes take time. Check in with your emotional guidance system – how do you feel about your dreams now? Feeling encouraged is recommended. Think the best thing you can about whatever you want. Feel good. Count your blessings.

If you're Moon-sensitive, this is the time of the month when you'll feel quite wound up and anxious. That's because, on some level, your body knows that this is the climax of your current cycle and that whatever you haven't quite managed to manifest may have to wait. This part of the cycle is yang – the energy is out there and our feelings are on display for all to see. Use this part of the cycle to release and let go. If something hasn't worked out, bless it and instead be grateful for all the good in your life.

Look back over the past month, too, and become conscious of anyone or anything that's hurt you. This isn't the time for blame, though: it's the time to forgive. When you forgive, you release the karma and when you do that, you exit the situation. And because nature abhors a vacuum, you need to replace what you're releasing. The idea is to use this high point in the lunar cycle to let go and move on.

Forgiveness is one of the most important gifts we can give ourselves. Truly! Because when we forgive, we can move on. Forgiving anyone or anything that's hurt you in the past four weeks (or indeed ever) is one of the healthiest things you can do for yourself – it's detoxifying. The clearer you are now, the better able you'll be to sow more seeds at the time of the New Moon in two weeks' time.

Once you've released any upset through forgiveness, fill up again with gratitude. The Full Moon is the time when emotions come to the surface to be dealt with. Once you've let go of any unsettled or unresolved feelings you have about someone or something, focus on good feelings by thinking about who and what you're grateful for. You'll learn more about New Moon forgiveness and gratitude in Part III.

The Disseminating Moon phase

- B-r-e-a-t-h-e...
- This phase begins 3½–7 days after the Full Moon.
- Keywords of this phase: *cycle: relax, accept, regroup*

After all the intensity of the Full Moon, it can be tempting to fall into a slump. If things didn't work out for you then, what next? A lot of energy has been expended and you may want to relax a little during this part of the cycle. If that's the case for you, then do it. You'll find that the more you work in accordance with the lunar phases, the more easily life will flow.

This isn't the time to start something new, then, but rather to go easy on yourself as you regroup your forces. The more you can accept 'what is', the better your emotional health. Also, the more you can down tools now, the greater your chances of success will be later on.

This is also a good time to share your wisdom with others. What have you learned? Can you pass it on? Over the past few weeks, you've been growing in wisdom and experience. Now is the time to share what you know with others.

We're now officially in the 'waning' phase. The Moon will appear to grow smaller every night between now and its disappearance at the time of the New Moon. It's as though we've stepped through from one side of life to another. We're through the door of the Full Moon and now we get to see what's on the other side.

Accept that you're where you are and it's okay. Try to relax during this part of the cycle. If you've been doing the hard yards on manifesting your dreams in the fortnight between the New Moon and the Full Moon, you'll have earned a break.

The Third Quarter Moon phase

- What do you know?
- This phase begins 7–10½ days after the Full Moon.
- Keywords of this phase: *re-evaluate, balance, trust*

This Moon phase can be awkward. It's the halfway point between the wonder of the Full Moon and the potential of the New Moon. On some level, we know that what didn't work for us in the past has dissolved on an etheric level. It's time to reorientate ourselves. Although we might feel tired during this part of the cycle, this is no time to stop, or to rest on our laurels. There's tension at this time: a result of the hard angle between the egotistical Sun and the emotional Moon.

We may not want to let go but we know we need to. *Adjustments are required.* We have to make way for the new, which we sense is just around the corner, in the form of the New Moon in one week's time. The Third Quarter Moon (like the First Quarter Moon) looks like a Half Moon. Any conflict that occurs now is worth examining – ask yourself what the message is in any challenges you face during this phase. A change of course may be called for. Let go.

This part of the cycle can be a crossroads. Look back and see how far you've come. Do you deserve a pat on the back for what you've achieved? Then allow yourself that. Where to from here? It can be decision time as you work out what you want to take with you into the New Moon cycle that's coming soon, and what you want to leave behind. This is also a very good time to break bad habits. You're at a turning point so the question is, 'Which way do you want to turn?' Are you sticking with your old plans or making new ones?

The Balsamic Moon phase

- And release...
- This phase begins around 10½ days after the Full Moon, and continues until just before the beginning of the New Moon.
- Keywords of this phase: *healing, soothing, surrender*

The word 'balsamic' comes from the word 'balsam', which means 'anything healing or soothing'. And that's what this 'last part' of the lunar cycle (before the New Moon) is all about. We've moved from hopes and dreams to explosions of potential: to realizations of what can and cannot be, to acceptance and forgiveness and surrender... and now comes the healing and the soothing.

If you want to live consciously, in line with the Moon cycles, this is the time to go easy on yourself. Start to think about your dreams again and allow hope to guide and inspire you. Remember that anything is possible. Live gently. B-r-e-a-t-h-e.

One of the best ways to work with this cycle is to chant the Sanskrit words '*Om Namo Narayani*', which is pronounced 'Om Na-moe Na-rye-Annee' and means 'I surrender to the Divine.' The Divine has a plan for us all, and we're all the Divine made manifest! So surrender now. It's easier said than done, but by chanting '*Om Namo Narayani*' and asking your soul to surrender, it becomes possible.

The lunar cycle is ending and it's really time to let go and move on. It's also a time for rest and healing. Give yourself a break. Daydream. Dream big. Go wild in your imagination. Smile to yourself. Once again, this is a brilliant time to put a stop to any habits that aren't good for you. It's also a time to end relationships that aren't working for you. If there has been a drama with someone and you want to continue the relationship, this is another wonderful time to release upset.

The Dark Moon phase

- Go deep into your psyche.
- This phase happens just before the New Moon.
- Keywords of this phase: *meditate, contemplate, release*

The mysterious dark phase of the Moon, when the Moon is unseen, takes place at the liminal time just before the New Moon. You could call it the very end of the lunar cycle, the last part of the Balsamic Moon phase, or the time just before the New Moon.

To the ancients, the Moon's monthly cycle represented the life, death and rebirth paradigm; the Full Moon was life, the New Moon was rebirth... and the Dark Moon was symbolically associated with death, endings and transition. In terms of Moonology and manifesting, it's a potent time when we aim to transition from the old to the new, from the waning to the waxing, from what we're leaving behind to what we want to create.

It's a time to withdraw. Allow time for introspection. Go deep into your psyche to see which doubts and fears are lurking and holding you back from reaching your potential. Be as honest with yourself as you can about what is between you and your dreams, be they large or small.

Clear out any lingering negativity and allow time for healing to raise your vibration ahead of the New Moon. Then you'll sound like a clear, ringing bell you when you send your New Moon wishes and intentions out into the universe.

Note that the Dark Moon phase is strongly connected to the Dark Goddesses; my favourite three to work with at this time are Kali, Lilith and Nyx. Their uncompromising and powerful energies offer the courage we need to face hidden aspects of our beliefs about ourselves, which could be holding us back.

It's a magical time to connect with your powers. It's the dark of the dark of the dark. The place where no one else can see you. You could also call it simply; the dark before the dawn.

When Moonology meets neuroscience

In the 10 years since *Moonology*™ was first published, it's been extraordinary to see how modern neuroscience has begun to explain what ancient mystics have long intuited – that our thoughts, emotions and intentions move in cycles.

The Moon's phases seemingly mirror the way the brain grows, prunes and resets. Every New Moon intention, Full Moon release and Dark Moon surrender aligns with how our minds rewire themselves through focus, action and letting go.

As the late Dr James Doty (1955–2025), author of *Mind Magic*, explained, when our attention is intentionally focused on what we want and why, change is possible.

Moonology, it turns out, isn't just
mystical – it's measurable.

In Moonology, we move not just from New Moon to Full Moon and back, but through a full spiritual and neurological cycle. Dr Doty tells us that the power to manifest lies not in wishing per se but in the interplay of intention, attention, emotion and action – exactly the cycle the Moon teaches us to follow. Let's look at this in more detail.

At the New Moon

In Moonology, the New Moon marks the moment to set intentions – to write our wishes, visualize our goals and begin again. Focused intention can strengthen emerging neural pathways, especially when paired with repeated visualization and action. As neuroscience in general, and Dr Doty in particular, explains, when we engage in visualization practices, we're teaching the brain 'to become intimately acquainted with our desires so that it recognizes them instantly'. Only after significant repetition can a desire become comfortable to the brain. The act of visualizing your goal activates the same brain areas as achieving it, triggering the dopaminergic reward circuitry (the part of the brain that motivates us to keep moving forwards).

Once we've set our intentions, another fascinating process begins: the Reticular Activating System (RAS) kicks in. This is part of the mind's internal filter, which sorts through the flood of information we receive every second and highlights what's most relevant to our current focus.

When you make your New Moon wishes, your RAS effectively tunes your awareness, helping you notice signs, synchronicities and opportunities that align with your intentions. What we often interpret as the Universe sending us messages is also this powerful neurological system showing us where our energy and attention are in sync.

Working in harmony with the salience network (the part of the brain that flags what's most important or relevant) helps you shift your attention to what matters right now. It's the mind's version of turning towards lunar light in the darkness.

This is why all good manifesting teachers tell you to pay attention to the signs that your manifesting is working. It's also why the example of manifesting from a broken-down old bike to a shiny new Mercedes (*see page 36*) works – because you can see that what you're doing is working.

During the Waxing Moon

As the Moon begins to wax, it's time to take action. In Moonology, this is the 'go for it' phase when we move towards our intentions and start making things happen. Once you've set your goal, your brain's salience network highlights opportunities, while the prefrontal cortex (the part that plays a key role in planning and decision-making) helps you follow through. In an interview with the University of Chicago,* Dr Doty says, 'It's great to have an idea, but unless you have somebody in charge making it happen, it's not going to happen.' Every time you take inspired action, the dopaminergic system (a group of brain cells that use dopamine to guide motivation, reinforcement and parts of how we think and act) rewards you, reinforcing confidence and faith in the process.

At the First Quarter Moon

This is the time in Moonology when things can feel tense, or crises or challenges often appear – not to stop you, but to help you grow. In *Mind Magic*, Doty notes, '…you may encounter what you believe you desire, but be surprised by a strong sensation of fear that's prompting you to push away what you thought you wanted.

* The University of Chicago (2024), 'How to manifest your future using neuroscience, with James Doty': https://news.uchicago.edu/manifest-your-future-using-neuroscience-james-doty [Accessed 1 December 2025]

This, too, isn't unusual, because fear is the brain's way of guarding against the novelty of experiencing your desire.' That fear comes from the amygdala (the brain's emotional alarm system), which flares when we step into the unknown. By staying calm and centred, you teach the amygdala that expansion is safe, allowing the executive functions of your prefrontal cortex to stay in charge. Each time you work through fear, you're literally rewiring your brain for courage and resilience. So, at the Quarter Moon, push through your fears!

At the Full Moon

As you now know, this is the time to forgive and release. It's when we surrender what no longer serves us, celebrate progress and make peace with the past. Emotional-healing research shows that forgiveness reduces stress and improves heart health. Doty adds, 'Only when we have shifted into the rest-and-digest response of the nervous system will our brains allow us to reclaim our attention, access the power of our imagination and unlock our subconscious.'

At this phase, the parasympathetic nervous system (the part of the nervous system that regulates rest functions) takes over, slowing the heart, lowering cortisol and activating healing. The limbic system (governs emotion and memory) integrates those shifts, while mirror neurons strengthen empathy and compassion. When we forgive or offer kindness, these neurons fire in harmony, reinforcing love and connection.

This is where the effect on manifesting begins. When we release resentment, our nervous system moves from protection into creation. The energy tied up in stress becomes available for intuition, imagination and inspired action – the very ingredients that bring our intentions to life. Letting go clears the emotional 'static' in the limbic system, allowing the brain's motivation and reward circuits to become active again. This is why forgiveness isn't just emotional housekeeping; it's a powerful manifesting tool. By freeing ourselves from the past, we make space in both our hearts and our minds for new blessings to arrive.

During the Disseminating Moon

As the Moon begins to wane, we enter the letting-go phase. In Moonology, this is when we release attachments and simplify. Neuroscience calls this neural pruning – the process of clearing away old synaptic pathways so the brain can form new ones. 'This superpower, moulded by experience, repetition and intention, enables the brain to form new circuits, and to prune away old ones which no longer serve us,' says Dr Doty. Letting go isn't just an emotional or spiritual act – it's biological. The brain itself evolves through this same process of renewal.

At the Last Quarter Moon

In Moonology, this is when we pause to make peace with what is, reflect on lessons and integrate what we've learned. In the brain, this corresponds with the Default Mode Network (DMN), the system that activates during rest and introspection, helping us make sense of our experiences. As Viktor Frankl is credited with saying, 'Between stimulus and response there's a space. In that space is our power to choose.' This is the essence of conscious integration, where the DMN and the prefrontal cortex work together to transform experience into wisdom.

At the Dark Moon

In Moonology, this is the time to retreat – to pause, meditate, release and clear space for the next cycle. Calm states allow the brain to integrate change. The parasympathetic nervous system deepens this rest, while the DMN quietly organizes memory and meaning. As Doty's research shows, compassion and stillness aren't just spiritual tools – they're neurological ones. The Dark Moon mirrors the brain's own need for pause and renewal: the sacred emptiness before creation begins again.

I wasn't lucky enough to interview Dr Doty before he passed away in 2025, so I don't know what he thought about astrology. I do know, however, that Moonology gives us the poetry, the ritual and the rhythm, and I believe that neuroscience explains why it works. Together they reveal that when we live in sync with the Moon – setting intentions, taking action, forgiving and letting go – we're also reshaping our minds, our hearts and our future. The changing Moon reflects the brain's own rhythm of transformation. She always has.

Summary

So now you have an overview of how to connect with the Moon. In this section you learned that:

- The Moon can be used as a magical cosmic timer to help you create your ideal life.
- Connecting with the Moon puts us in touch with Her cycles and rhythms.
- There are nine major Moon phases and the New Moon and Full Moon are the lunar cycle's high points.
- The New Moon is the time to put your wishes and intentions out there to the Universe.
- The Full Moon is a time when we can become extra emotional, which makes sense, as the Moon can influence our mood and feelings.

FAQs: the Moon and Her phases

Before we go any further, I thought I'd address some of the more general questions I'm often asked about the Moon and Her phases.

Astrologically, what do New/Full Moons mean?

I have a personal theory that the New Moon is when we humans get a tad weirded-out because we know that change is afoot, and many of us aren't that keen on change. Moreover, on a primal level, I believe that some part of us freaks out when we can't see the Moon – and we can't see the Moon when she's new.

The big and round Full Moon is seen as the climax of the monthly lunar cycle. Yes, size matters! The Moon seemingly swells as we reach the peak of the cycle. After that, it's time to let go, release, and move on, as the Moon becomes more and more of a slim sliver until it temporarily disappears. (The New Moon rises and sets with the Sun.)

As I mentioned earlier, astrologically, the Moon is associated with feelings (among other things). So it makes symbolic sense that, as the Moon grows fuller, so do our feelings. Which is why, at the peak of the lunar cycle – the Full Moon – we humans are renowned for getting a bit emotional. You also need to know that:

- The New Moon is dark and hidden and associated with witches; it's all about secrecy and veiled mysteries.
- The Full Moon is associated with the round, swollen, gorgeous and illuminating Goddess.

What's a Void-of-Course Moon?

To answer this, I first need to give you some very basic information about astrology. As you know, astrologers study the planets' movements, and what that means is that we study the angles – or 'aspects' – that the planets are making to each other. So for example, when two planets are 90° away from each other on the 360° wheel of the skies/astrological chart, they're said to be making a 'square' (which is a clashing angle – aspect – that can cause issues to come up for dealing with).

When two planets are 60° apart, they're said to be making a sextile (an easier aspect); 120° apart is a trine (easy) and 0° (which is when the planets are in the same place at the same time) is a conjunction (they can go either way, depending). When planets are 180° apart they're oppositions, which are challenging.

With that said, here are three main definitions of a Void-of-Course (VOC) Moon:

1. The Moon doesn't make an aspect with any planet until it moves into the next sign of the zodiac.
2. The Moon doesn't make an exact aspect with any planet within the next 30° of its travels.
3. The Moon isn't making an exact aspect within a 10° orb.

The first definition is by far the most widely used and that's the one you should be concerned with. *It's said that whatever we start when the Moon is VOC will bear no fruit.* This is definitely not the time to start a new business or plan a wedding. It's a time just to 'be': to meditate and practise yoga, if you can. Note that having a VOC Moon in your astrological birth chart isn't the same thing, and is a topic beyond the scope of this book.

What's a Supermoon?

A Supermoon is a New or Full Moon that closely coincides with perigee – aka the Moon's closest point to Earth in Her monthly orbit. There are 4–6 Supermoons a year. They're more impactful if they affect your own personal Moon on your birth chart.

What's a Blue Moon?

'Once in a Blue Moon'... no book about the Moon would be complete without a mention of Blue Moons. There are usually three Full Moons between an equinox and a solstice (or vice versa). Sometimes, though, four Full Moons fall in a single season. When that happens, the third of a season's four Full Moons is called a Blue Moon.

That was the original definition of a Blue Moon, but another has since been ascribed to it: A Blue Moon can also be the second Full Moon in a calendar month with two Full Moons; this happens far more often. Neither type of Blue Moon has any particular astrological significance.

Note that sometimes we get two consecutive Full Moons in the same sign, but these aren't officially known as Blue Moons. However, this rare occurrence does have astrological significance; it's like a double-whammy 'call to action' in your birth chart.

What's a Black Moon?

There are several definitions for a Black Moon. It's the third New Moon in a season (spring, summer, autumn or winter) with four New Moons; the second New Moon in a calendar month; or the absence of a Full or New Moon in a calendar month.

When is the best time to...

Cut your hair at the time of the Balsamic Moon if you don't want it to grow back too quickly. Ditto fingernails, weeds and plants. Think about which seeds you want to plant in the garden at the time of the upcoming New Moon. Surgery will be less traumatic at this time too, with less blood loss. Plus, you have the New Moon around the corner to boost healing.

Where do eclipses come into it?

A New Moon eclipse is a solar eclipse and a Full Moon eclipse is a lunar eclipse. If you have a New Moon eclipse or Full Moon eclipse in a certain part of your chart, you get the usual New Moon or Full Moon effects plus plus!

Eclipses open up portals to another future in the part of our life being triggered. It's up to us to jump through these – or not. The Universe changes gears, and we get shoved back onto our right and proper path by events, whether we're ready or not.

Suffice it to say that back in ye olden days, eclipses were feared. The skies would grow dark, the dogs would start howling and quite understandably, people would freak out. Afterwards, they would blame pretty much anything bad that had happened during the eclipse on 'that perilous day the skies went dark'.

These days we can predict when eclipses will take place, so no one is taken by surprise by them. And indeed, most modern astrologers see eclipses as amazing portents of potential change. Think of it like this: You came to Earth with a job to do. Basically, your soul has some kind of mission, and your life has a purpose. However, it's all too easy for us humans to listen to our ego and not to our soul.

We can easily get distracted and sidetracked by life (and love) and before we know it, we've wandered off our path. That's usually when life feels really hard. We know we're not living the way we should. We get entangled in toxic relationships or caught up in draining jobs. We're NOT in the flow!

And then? Along come the eclipses and we get shunted back to where we're meant to be. It really is that simple. The trouble is, sometimes our egos aren't happy about these unscheduled life changes. What happens at the time of an eclipse can be oh so challenging. And yet they pretty much always work out for the best. (The way to make an eclipse easier is to avoid hanging on to the past.)

PART II

Create Your Dream Life with The New Moon

Working with the Moon when you're manifesting is a key to its success. While in theory you can manifest your dreams any time, anywhere, with the right intentions and commitment, doing your 'manifesting work' in tune with the Moon supercharges your dreams.

CHAPTER 3

New Moon Manifesting

Now we come to one of the most exciting parts of the book: New Moon manifesting. You're about to learn how to do a very powerful practice.

Essentially, New Moon manifesting reminds us to get clear on our dreams and goals once a month – and write them down or draw them. I like to call this process 'making my New Moon wishes'. However, some people find the idea of 'making wishes' a bit wishy-washy, and prefer to say they're 'setting intentions' – which does sound more adult and businesslike.

Personally, I see wishes and intentions as quite different things, but they actually go together well. I like to make wishes and set my intentions for the month ahead. I also like the idea of making a New Moon *commitment*.

The labels you give to your New Moon Manifesting aren't really important. It's up to you. The main thing is that you feel good about them and that *you do them*. As I said, though, overall I prefer the idea of making 'wishes', so that's mainly what I'll call them in this chapter.

The secret of New Moon Manifesting

The secret to making wishes or setting intentions is to ensure that they *come from the heart, and that you feel them as if they've already happened*. Read that again. The secret to making wishes or setting intentions is to ensure that they *come from the heart, and that you feel them as if they've already happened.*

This is something many people don't understand. We can repeat affirmations and make vision boards ad infinitum, but if we don't wish from the heart and *feel as if we've already received what we're wishing for*, we're wasting our time. It's crucial that you really 'get' this straight off the mark. Other keys to successful wishing are to:

- Fake it 'til you make it. In other words, pretend to yourself that your dreams have already come true. Feel the feeling of the wish fulfilled. Revel in that feeling.
- Think about what you *do* want; don't think about what you *don't* want. This is a golden rule. Just do it.
- Write down or draw what you *do* want; forget about what you *don't* want.

We humans aren't always aware of how powerful we are. But once we start to connect with the Moon and work with the lunar cycles, our power becomes mind-blowingly obvious. Perhaps the most important thing to remember about making New Moon wishes is that *you can't get what you want until you know what you want*. It's simply the way life works.

When we're *really clear* about what we want, it makes it much easier for us to make it happen, with the conspiring help of the Universe. In fact, what we're doing when we make wishes/set intentions at the monthly New Moon is getting really, really clear on what we want. In the same way that a shopping list helps us to shop, writing a wish list of 'what we want' helps us to manifest.

What if I Don't Know What I Want?

This is a really hard one – and the answer lies in 'going within'. Ask the Universe, God, Goddess, your higher self, your Archangels and guides – whoever you feel can help you – for guidance so that you get clarity. And/or ask yourself: 'What do I want?' Ask this repeatedly as you go about your day, or at the start or end of your meditations. The answer will come if you persist: Pay attention to the messages, thoughts and ideas that filter through. Or if you don't feel you can do it alone, ask for a new spiritual teacher to come into your life.

~

New Moon wishing: the golden rules

Before I show you how to make your New Moon wishes, I'd like to share the golden rules that I've developed around the process over the years: these work well for me and for the thousands of people I've taught. I can't say categorically that if you don't adhere to the following 'dos and don'ts' your wishes won't work, but as you'll see, the overall idea is to wish for good things for yourself and for other people.

Do wish for anything you want

You can wish for anything you want, and as long as you believe you can have it, it can be yours.

Do take baby steps

Your wishes can be as wild as you like – if you can believe it, you can achieve it – but in that case, I find that it helps to take baby steps towards them. For example, during my New Moon wishing and intention-setting workshops, I invite participants to share their wishes with the group, and occasionally someone who doesn't yet have a job will write: 'I wish to own a house', or 'I wish to win the lottery.'

Now in the first example, my advice to the participant would be: 'First wish to find a job, so you can earn the money to buy a house.' And in the second example, I'd say: 'Well, you *can* wish to win the lottery, but I believe that in the back of your mind, you doubt that it will happen, as you know the odds are totally stacked against you. To put it another way, your odds of finding a job are much, much better. Having said that, you could always wish to find a job *and* to win the lottery!'

Let's look at a similar 'material' wish. Imagine that it's your dream to own a brand-new Mercedes, but right now, you have little cash available. It's hard to go from being broke to owning a Mercedes in one leap: not impossible, but pretty tricky. Remember, one of the secrets of New Moon wishing is simply to *believe* that what you're wishing for, or intending to do, is possible and within your reach. So in this example, we can break the wish down into baby steps:

Go from broke => owning a bicycle => owning an inexpensive second-hand car => owning a second-hand Mercedes => owning a brand-new Mercedes.

So my point is, achieving this particular dream will take time – and quite a few New Moons. There are practical things to be done on the journey from being broke to owning a brand-new Mercedes, and you can't just leapfrog them. To make it really clear: when we make wishes, we're manifesting – and that's magic – but unless we're incredibly gifted, we cannot simply override the laws of physics. And we're also limited by what we *believe* is possible.

As you start to manifest by New Moon wishing, you may attract close-but-no-cigar demonstrations, which shouldn't be ignored. Let's say that, having wished to get closer to owning a shiny new Mercedes, the next day, a brochure from Mercedes drops through your letterbox. Yes, it's a sign. It means you're getting closer to your dream. Or a friend asks you to 'mind' their Merc while they're on holiday. You're getting closer still. Patience and faith are most certainly required on this journey.

Do wish for a 'feeling'

But should you be wishing for a Mercedes (or any other material object) in the first place? It could be argued that wishing for 'stuff', be it a car, a house in the country, or anything else along those lines, is a deluded, greedy waste of your manifestation powers. Any super-rich person will tell you that owning things doesn't bring happiness. Sure, you might rejoice in your fantastic new 50-inch flatscreen TV for a few days but after that, it will more than likely become – literally – just a part of the furniture.

So in the long term, material possessions don't make us happy, right? Or wrong? Perhaps you're a stay-at-home person and nothing brings you greater joy than sitting with your cat, or your beloved, or your beloved and your kids, on the sofa on a Friday night and watching a movie on TV. In that case, is it okay to wish for a big screen on which to watch it?

I believe that as long as you realize that owning 'stuff' isn't what makes us happy, you can wish for whatever you want and ignore the naysayers. However, having said that, there's also truth in the idea that when we wish for, say, a big TV, what we're really wishing for is the *feeling* we get when we watch it. For some of us that could be the feeling that all the hard work we put in to earn the cash to buy the TV was worthwhile, or it could be the lovely feeling of happy times with the family that we're seeking.

So if you already know that what you want is to feel more positive about yourself, say, or to have an increased sense of self-worth, or to enjoy happier times at home with your family, then wish for *that feeling* rather than a 'thing'.

You can even do a bit of self-analysis as you look over your monthly New Moon wishes. What was your motivation for desiring something? Was it a feeling you were chasing, or a gap you were trying to fill? Ideally, you should let your wishes be extensions of your own *joie de vivre*. In other words, add-ons that will make you feel happier.

So, to sum up: is it really okay to wish for a huge, luxuriously appointed house in which to entertain family and friends? Yes, absolutely: provided that's what you *really* want. And as long as you're wishing for it because you *love* the thought of it – because it will make you happy.

But if your motivation for wishing for that big house stems from envy – from wanting what someone else has – that's not so good. For one thing, envy is unhealthy, so work on that. For another, envy blocks gratitude and we need to be grateful in order to manifest. The most important thing when you're wishing for anything is to be *grateful* for what you already have. More on that in a moment.

◗ Don't wish for a specific person

Is it okay to wish for someone else's partner – i.e. to have their girlfriend, boyfriend or spouse? Short answer: no. Can you wish for someone who *is* available? Yes, you can certainly ask for them to notice you, but at the end of the day, you must remember that we all have free will, so you can't just New-Moon-wish someone into your life. They have to want to be there.

One possible scenario, if you put enough energy into it, would be for you to manifest bumping into a particular person and then hold the intention to ask them out (and carry that out as well). But then of course it's up to the person whether or not they say 'yes'. Do you see what I mean?

What about wishing to hook up with Leonardo DiCaprio/Justin Bieber/Jennifer Lawrence? Yes, you can do this, provided you really believe it's possible – and provided there's just one degree of separation between you and them. Otherwise it's more than likely a waste of time, and a waste of a good New Moon wish.

◗ Don't wish for someone to change

Sadly perhaps, New Moon wishes can't magically transform a toad or toad-ette into a Prince or Princess Charming. It's really important that you understand this before you start on your manifesting quest. You can't turn a quintessential charming bad boy into a boy scout angel, unless he *wants* to turn into a boy scout angel. Same applies to 'bad' or 'dangerous' girls. New Moon manifesting can't interfere with someone else's free will.

All this applies triple if you're in an abusive relationship. Rather than wishing for your partner to change, wish instead for the courage to leave them. The bottom line is, *you* can't change people – they have to want to change themselves. It's a cliché that we so often ignore.

◗ Do believe that you're worthy of your wishes

One important question to ask yourself on a regular basis as you start to make your monthly New Moon wishes is: 'Do I think I'm worthy of what I'm wishing for?' It's a sad fact that many of us grew up with parents who weren't as supportive as they might have been, and as adults, we now wonder whether we're entitled to *anything.*

Ask yourself the following. Emotionally: Do you believe that you *deserve* the great friendships and relationships you're asking for in your wish lists? Financially: Do you believe that money is bad? (If you do, of course you won't attract it to you.)

Work with The Law of Intention and Desire

When you align with the New Moon to make your wishes, you're activating what teacher Deepak Chopra calls The Law of Intention and Desire, which states that 'the future is created in the present'.

There are lots of very clever people around who might try and argue against astrology, but even they would agree with Chopra's concept. I believe that the New Moon is a really wonderful marker that comes like clockwork once a month to remind us that it's time to get back in alignment with our desires and intentions.

~

Do meditate

When you come to use my guide to making New Moon wishes (below), you'll see that meditation is the crucial final step in the process. I'd like to explain here, before you start to get in the zone, why meditation is so important. The reason is simple: When we make New Moon wishes, we're manifesting. And being clear about what we want, and expressing it effectively, is so powerful.

Think of yourself as like a radio: When you make your wishes they're like radio waves that emanate from you; your wishes are your way of letting the Universe (which is benevolent and on your side!) know what you want. And when you meditate after making your wishes, the signal becomes even clearer, because meditation can decrease anxiety, make you happier and even restructure your brain in a really positive way. If you want proof of this, read on:

A 2011 study conducted in the USA by a Harvard University-affiliated team from Massachusetts General Hospital found that meditation actually alters the shape of the brain. Over an eight-week period, the study's participants spent an average of

27 minutes a day meditating. At the end of the study, MRI scans of the participants' brains showed that this had led to an increase in grey-matter density in the hippocampus – the part of the brain associated with learning, memory, self-awareness, compassion and introspection.

The participants also reported a reduction in stress, which correlated with a decrease in grey-matter density seen in the amygdala, a part of the brain that plays an important role in regulating anxiety and stress.

But what does this have to do with New Moon wishing? Well, the more relaxed and stress-free we are, the better we're able to manifest. It's not enough just to sit down and make your New Moon wishes once a month and then lead a chaotic life. Perhaps you find this surprising? Yet deep down, on some level, you bought this book because you knew you had to get this information.

Living a harmonious life – one in which we coexist with others in as beautiful a fashion as possible – is the way to bring in the lives we're dreaming of. You'll be amazed at the wonderful things that begin to happen once you start to check in with your Divine self – because that's essentially what you're doing when you meditate.

Your Divine self is the part of you that's still connected to Heaven, more or less. You may have read that we're 'multi-dimensional beings'. That's because we're here in the third dimension but still connected to our 'higher selves', which are in the higher dimensions. The more we connect with our Divine self or higher self, the better – and the more able we are to manifest our desires in this physical world.

With all that said, you might be wondering whether your New Moon wishes will work if you don't meditate? Probably, but the process will likely feel less graceful. Also, meditation will help you work out what you really want, rather than just making some flippant wish.

☾ How To Meditate in 9 Easy Steps

If you're new to meditation, here's a short guide to incorporating it into the New Moon wishing process. If you'd rather be guided in your meditation, you can access a free audio guide at moonmessages.com/easymeditation; YouTube has lots of great videos too. There are many ways to meditate, but essentially it's a simple process that will really help you to manifest your dreams.

Perform the following steps once or twice a day, for 15 minutes each time.

1. Turn off your phone and find somewhere comfortable and quiet to sit.
2. Close your eyes, and start to become aware of the rise and fall of your breath.
3. Listen to any sounds inside the room, and then return to listening to your breath.
4. Listen to any noises outside the room, and then return to listening to your breath.
5. Acknowledge any thoughts that arise, and then return to listening to your breath.
6. Bring a mantra[†] to mind and repeat it, silently or out loud.
7. After performing steps 1–6 for 15 minutes, think of someone or something you're really grateful for.
8. Ask yourself: 'What do I want?', and see what springs to mind.
9. Open your eyes, rub your hands together and place them over your face or heart.

~

* A mantra is a word or a sound that's repeated silently or out loud during meditation. The word 'Om' is the best known of them all.

Do 'release attachment' to your wishes

There's one last thing to be aware of before you begin to make your New Moon wishes: While it's important to get clear on what you really want, paradoxically, you shouldn't become too attached to your dreams. Because guess what – the Universe might have a better idea than the one you have in mind.

Have you ever noticed that sometimes in life, you might desperately want X but then Y happens and, unexpectedly, Y is better than X and everything turns out for the best? That's what happens when the Universe has a better idea! It's also why, once we've made our wishes, we release attachment to them by saying a phrase such as *For the good of all or not at all.* This tells the Universe that this is what you want, but only if it's for the good of all.

I always chant '*Om Namo Narayani*' after making my New Moon wishes. The words are Sanskrit – which is said to be both the oldest language in the world and the language of the Archangels – and mean 'I surrender to the Divine.' Or more specifically: 'I surrender to the Divine Mother'. After all, mother knows best.

You can chant *Om Namo Narayani* (which is pronounced 'Om Na-moe Na-rye-Annee'), or say it, or even think it, after making your wishes, or during or after your meditation. You can even scrawl it on your New Moon wishes and intentions list. When we affirm that we want something and then release attachment to it in this way, our wishes go out into the Universe and something as good, or better, comes back.

Releasing attachment certainly doesn't have to be something you do only at the time of the New Moon. You can do it every day. The less attached we are to things and people, the more our lives will flow. When we're obsessed with something (or someone) we create a sort of energetic anchor that keeps us stuck. Releasing the desire releases the anchor. Also note that being desperate for something often pushes it away. Unconsciously, when we crave someone or something, we're constantly affirming the fact that we *don't* have it. And the more we affirm that, the more we don't have it! It's the Law of Attraction at work.

So what's going on here? Are we making our New Moon wishes on the one hand and relinquishing all desire on the other? Actually, yes: I do believe that we create our own reality and that one of our challenges in this physical life is to create. Overriding that, though, I believe there's a higher power that guides us – whether we call it our higher self, the Creator, the Universe, the Source or God.

I believe that as long as we make our wishes perfectly clear to the Universe, and as long as we've fully and robustly imagined things happening as we'd like them to, then whatever *does* actually happen will be for our highest good.

It's very hard to cover all the bases at all times, and the Universe really does move in mysterious ways. I say the words *Om Namo Narayani*, safe in the knowledge that yes, the Divine Mother really does know best. It's part relinquishing responsibility, and part surrendering. Surrendering means trusting that the best thing will happen.

How to make New Moon wishes

To check the time of the next New Moon, visit my site – yasminboland.com – or the excellent timeanddate.com/moon/phases. Then follow these steps as soon as possible after the New Moon (ideally up to eight hours after it, but up to three days is okay too).

New Moon Wishing Step-by-Step

1. Start by setting the scene. You want to raise your vibration for this, so put on some beautiful spiritual music (*see page 249 for suggestions*), light a candle and some incense, or put

some oil in your diffuser, and centre yourself with a few deep, cleansing breaths.

2. Take a moment to feel gratitude for all that's good in your life. Then think about the people and situations that make you happiest. Write down everyone and everything for which you've been grateful in the past month, or ever. Feel gratitude for all this.
3. Now turn your mind to your wishes and/or intentions for the coming four weeks. What do you want to manifest? What do you want to create in your life? What are you calling in? If you like, you can visit moonmessages.com/NMworksheet to access a worksheet on which you can write your wish lists. You'll also find an audio guide to support you in the process.
4. Start by writing down your number one goal for the coming four weeks. Write as though it's already happening, for example, 'I'm so excited because...', and then write out your wish as though it's already coming true. As you write, 'feel the feeling of the wish fulfilled', as Wayne Dyer and his teacher Neville Goddard put it. *Feel* it as real. Imagine it. See it in your mind's eye. What does it look like and how do you feel in this new reality you're calling to you? Enjoy these feelings: they're what make the magic. Feel the joy you'd feel. Really see it. Feel the outcome in your body – feel what it's like for your wish to come true.
5. Now create an affirmation that backs up your wish and write that down too. For example, if you're wishing for love you could write, 'I'm so happy I'm in love!' Or, if you want to make a career change: 'I love my new job!' Write out your affirmation and say it silently or out loud – you'll need to say it to yourself all month between now and the Full Moon when you'll release it to the Universe. Make it a jaunty, snappy ditty: 'I love my new home!', 'I've found an amazing new source of income and I feel GREAT!', 'I am loved, loving and lovable!'

6. Next, think of ways to ground this dream and make it happen. For example, if your wish is to find a new job, your first step towards that could be to network or look at adverts on job sites. Or if you want to meet a partner, two obvious first steps would be to ask friends to set you up with someone, or sign up to a dating app. Write down how you intend to achieve your wish.
7. Repeat steps 4–6 for up to three wishes. Note, we used to say 10 wishes, but the intervening years have shown me that three is plenty! Do more if you feel you can handle it.
8. Finally, meditate for 15 minutes to release your dreams to the Universe. You can follow my meditation guide (see *page 42*) and/or access some free post-meditation audio at moonmessages.com/easymeditation.
9. End your meditation by releasing attachment to your wishes. Do this by saying, 'For the good of all or not at all!' and/or chanting '*Om Namo Narayani*' (Om Na-moe Na-rye-Annee) three times, which means 'I surrender to the Divine'. Or just say, 'This or something better now manifests for me, under grace in perfect ways.' Say it with a happy and confident flourish – feel as though it's happening, or at the very least strongly anticipate it!
10. You can now either safely burn your list or put it somewhere you can find it later. Burning releases your attachment to it and is more powerful, but if you're left-brained like me, it's great to be able to refer back to a list. Either way, you can get on with the rest of your week, safe in the knowledge that you've expressed your wishes to the Universe. Say your affirmation as often as you can – while you shower, do the dishes, travel to work – whenever! Believe it. And do everything practical you can to make your wishes come true.

~

Summary

Here's a quick, easy-to-use summary of the New Moon wishing process:

- **Write down** your **top three wishes** for the month.
- **Visualize and feel** your wishes in your body. Write down an affirmation to support them.
- **Write down** how you **intend** to work towards making each wish happen.
- **Meditate,** and then **release attachment** to your wishes by saying, 'For the good of all or not at all!' and/or '*Om Namo Narayani*'.

Focus, Focus, Focus

Really want something? Commit to doing at least 68 seconds of full-on visualization and feeling of having it *every day, or twice a day,* and you'll surely start to create it. A really effective way to do this is to write affirmation 'lines' – a bit like in the old days when schoolkids were made to write the same sentence over and again. Write out your affirmation dozens of times.

I did this exercise once when our holiday flights were cancelled because of a natural disaster in the country we were planning to visit. Initially we were told that we fell just outside the window for refunds, so I spent a good hour writing the following sentence, over and over again, feeling it as real:

'I am so delighted that we got a full refund for our flights and hotel!'

And guess what? We got a full refund for our flights and hotel!

Try this with your most important monthly New Moon affirmation. Writing it down makes it easier to stay really focused for that all-important 68 seconds. Imagine you're telling a friend your good news as you write.

~

New Moon wishing examples

Below are some tips for putting the wishing/visualization/affirmation/intention stages together. 'I am…' is an especially powerful phrase to use in an affirmation. Whenever you can, turn your affirmation around to start with the words 'I am…'.

Example 1: You'd like a new car

Your *wish* could be:

- 'I wish to own a new car' – to which you could add a brand name or other details, such as colour or horsepower, or electric windows, or manual or automatic.

Your *visualization* could be:

- Seeing yourself driving around in your new car, perhaps with the window wound down and the radio playing – whatever would thrill you.
- If you want the car in order to drive your kids around, see them sitting in the back seat, smiling and behaving nicely.
- Something that would feel good – for example, offering someone a lift to the airport in your new car or picking up a friend from the shops.

Your *affirmation* could be:

- 'I am loving my fantastic new car!'
- 'I am driving my awesome new car!'
- 'I have found my perfect car!'

Your *intention* and/or *commitment* could be:

- 'I intend to ask my friends if they know someone with a car to sell.'
- 'I intend to look at online car advertisements.'
- 'I commit to setting money aside each week to pay for the things associated with my new car, such as insurance.'

Remember *to really feel the feeling of having your wish fulfilled.* Are you starting to see how this works?

Here are a few more examples.

Example 2: You're unhappily single

Your *wish* could be:

- 'I wish to find a new lover or partner.'
- 'I wish to have more love options.'
- 'I wish to find a husband or wife.'

Your *visualization* could be:

- Seeing yourself on a date with your beloved. How does that *feel* in your body?
- Imagining yourself walking down the aisle with your beloved (if marriage appeals!).
- Noticing how you feel, both energetically and spiritually. Tasting the joy and the love.

Your *affirmation* could be:

- 'I am so excited to have found a partner!'
- 'I am in love with my beloved!'
- 'I am with my perfect partner.'

Your *intention* and/or *commitment* could be:

- 'I intend to look after my body so I can feel really good about myself.'
- 'I commit to getting out and about, or going online, to increase my love chances.'
- 'I intend to spend a few minutes every day visualizing myself happy in the arms of my new lover.'

Example 3: You want to lose weight

Your *wish* could be:

- 'I wish to drop X kilos/pounds.'
- 'I wish to fit into a size 10 dress.'
- 'I wish to be in top physical condition.'

Your *visualization* could be:

- Seeing yourself wearing a dress in your ideal size.
- Imagining yourself out with friends, dressed in clothes you'd love to wear.
- Noticing how you feel, both energetically and spiritually. So light and agile.

Your *affirmation* could be:

- 'I am so excited to have lost X kilos/pounds.'
- 'I am loving my new figure!'
- 'I am the perfect size for me!'

Your *intention* and/or *commitment* could be:

- 'I intend to exercise for at least 20 minutes every day.'

- 'I intend to eat smaller portions at mealtimes.'
- 'I commit to eating healthier food.'

◗ Example 4: You'd like to achieve success at work

Your *wish* could be:

- 'I wish to find a great internship that will kick-start my career.'
- 'I wish to find a great new job.'
- 'I wish to own and run my own company.'

Your *visualization* could be:

- Seeing yourself behaving with confidence in a job interview.
- Imagining yourself walking through the front door of the company of your dreams.
- Seeing yourself performing the tasks associated with your ideal job.
- Noticing how you feel, both energetically and spiritually. Tasting the joy and the passion.

Your *affirmation* could be:

- 'I am so excited to have found a job!'
- 'I am loving my new job!'
- 'I am so good at my new job!'

Your *intention* and/or *commitment* could be:

- 'I intend to look on job sites for a position that appeals to me.'
- 'I will polish my CV and update my wardrobe, so I impress in interviews.'
- 'I intend to research company X before I apply for a job there.'

- 'I commit to spending a few minutes every day visualizing myself working in the company of my choice.'

Commit with your mind, body and spirit:

- **Think** it in your mind.
- **Feel** it in your body.
- **Revel** in it in your spirit.

FAQs: New Moon wishing

Here's some more detailed information about the New Moon wishing process.

What should I do with my wish list afterwards?

Anything you like, really! However, one school of thought says that once we've written our wish lists, we should burn them (safely!). I do like this idea, as it's quite dramatic. Moreover, it's said that when we burn our wish lists, we release the energy of them (yes, of course wishes have energy) into the ether, where they can be transmuted into reality. To me, this makes total sense on an energetic level.

And nothing says 'release attachment to my New Moon wish list' like burning the list. If you do decide to burn yours, do it over the kitchen sink, so you don't set fire to the house in the process! You can also rip up your lists, which has the effect of making you forget your wishes once you've made them.

However, I write my wishes in a little booklet, purely because I'm the kind of person who likes proof. There's nothing like finding some old New Moon wishes in a notebook a few weeks, months or even years later, and seeing how many of them came true.

◗ Can I make a wish for someone else?

Yes, you can; however, there are two things to bear in mind. Firstly, why aren't you wishing for yourself? Is there truly nothing in your life that you want to create or improve? Do you feel that you aren't worthy of your wishes? That question needs to be answered. It's lovely to think of others, but it's also important to think of, and honour, ourselves.

Secondly, we need to remember that we can make all the wishes we like for someone else, but if it's not what they want for themselves, there's nothing we can do to change that – nor should we try. Of course, if you and a friend agree that you'll make the same wishes for one or both of you, then that will amplify the power.

◗ What can I do if my wishes aren't coming true?

If you wish and wish for something and your wish doesn't come true – and you don't seem to be edging in the right direction either – then it's time to consider whether it's the right thing for you. I once received an email from a reader who'd been wishing for the love of his life to fall in love with him for more than a year, and still she wasn't interested. In his case, I believed a rethink was needed.

Some things aren't meant to be. This is why we say, 'For the good of all or not at all!' or '*Om Namo Narayani*' after making our wishes – we trust that the Universe has our best interests at heart. I once applied for a job that I thought I really wanted – a wonderfully well-paid gig at a magazine. At the same time, I was also in the running for an online gig that was also great, but paid much less. I said '*Om Namo Narayani*' and ended up with the online job. The magazine folded shortly afterwards, but the online job is still running, many years later.

◗ Should I write 'I want…' or 'I wish…'?

You can phrase your wishes in any way that feels right for you – there's no secret formula that you must get right. The most important thing is to get clear on *what you want* – once you've done that, you're halfway there. And the most important things after that are to write down your wishes, to feel the feeling of having them come true, and to check back in with yourself a month later – to see how you've fared with them.

◗ Can I make my wishes with other people?

Yes you can! In fact, it's actually a great practice to get into, because the group energy can really boost your manifestation powers. I often hold New Moon Manifesting nights in whichever city I'm in on the night that follows the New Moon. You can find details of these on my site, yasminboland.com.

Or you could throw a New Moon wishing party. On the night that follows the New Moon, ask a friend or a few friends over, serve up some snacks and then follow the step-by-step New Moon wishing guide above – use coloured pens and pencils to make your wish lists even more gorgeous. (Note that the New Moon can take place morning, noon or night… the best time to make your wishes is as soon as possible after it.)

◗ Does my personal astrology affect my wishes?

Yes. One thing you may not have considered is the fact that your personal astrology can affect your ability to manifest. If you're already an astrologer, or a student astrologer, it's worth bearing in mind that what you have in your birth chart and what you have going on by transit at any one time can of course influence and affect your ability to manifest at the time of the New Moon.

For example, if you have depressing Saturn on your Sun, it's possible you'll have less self-belief that you can create your dream life. As all astrologers know, Saturn can bring a lot of negativity and self-doubt. However, Saturn is also about building something that's real and durable, so aim to turn all aspects of your birth chart and current transits into positives for manifesting.

◗ Does it matter if I'm in the northern or southern hemisphere?

No. Although the Moon will look different, or appear to face different directions depending on where you are on Earth, a New Moon is a New Moon and it's great for manifesting!

CHAPTER 4

Plan Your Life with the New Moon

So now you know how to make wishes at the time of the New Moon. That can and will change your life. But wait: there's more amazing work to be done at this Moon phase! You can also tune into the New Moon every month to get more in the cosmic flow. In other words, you can work with the celestial energies.

How the zodiac signs 'flavour' the New Moon

Each New Moon falls in one sign of the zodiac or another, and as a result, each New Moon acquires a certain 'flavour' as it takes on the qualities of the sign. For example, Gemini is a very chatty sign, so when we get the Moon in Gemini, the vibe is chattier. The New Moon in Gemini is a wonderful time to focus on what we're saying, how well we're listening, how effectively we're getting our message across and so on.

Meanwhile, the New Moon in Virgo has a real tidy-up feel to it (Virgo loves a good tidy-up). It's a wonderful time to get yourself organized. And the New Moon in Capricorn is a great time to sort out your career and ambitions (Capricorn is a very ambitious sign).

There's a full guide to the New Moon in each sign coming up, but basically what you need to understand is that each New Moon brings energies that we can use. Tuning in to these energies is a part of what it means to 'live consciously': being aware of the energies tunes us in to the cosmos.

The following box provides more information for the more technically minded among you – if you prefer, you can skip this.

The New Moon Through The 12 Signs

The New Moon takes place when the Sun and the Moon are on the same degree of the zodiac at the same time. The Sun takes a month to move through one sign and 12 months to move through all 12 signs. In comparison, the speedy Moon takes just two and a bit days to move through each sign and a month to move through all 12.

This means that once a month, the Moon catches up with the Sun and we get the New Moon. So for example, when your Cancerian friends are celebrating their birthdays, it means the Sun is in Cancer and the New Moon in Cancer will happen. The same goes for all 12 signs.

~

You don't need any in-depth astrological information to find out which sign the Moon is in: just ask Google, or check your online news feed if you follow any astrologers.

A guide to the New Moon in each sign

Below is a guide to **the top 5 things to do** at the time of the New Moon in each sign. If you plan your life by the New Moon, you'll find you're in the flow of life. Note that the advice in the guide applies to *all of us*, regardless of our personal astrology. The reason is, this is a lunation – in this case a New Moon – in a particular sign, and it therefore has a flavour of its own, no matter which star sign or rising sign we are.

The idea is to connect with all 12 New Moons so you work magic in pretty much every part of your life: the New Moon and the Laws of Attraction and Intention make excellent bedfellows.

Also note that in all cases, you can apply the following New Moon information to a solar, aka New Moon, eclipse. To explain further, imagine that the New Moon is in Aries, which means it's a good time of the year for us to work on our courage – to be braver and not timid. However, a New Moon eclipse in Aries means it's not just a good idea, it's a really, really good idea, or even crucial somehow! Eclipses are like New Moons on steroids. They're definitely worth following through the signs and through the Houses in your chart (we'll cover that later).

Please note: the months shown beneath each New Moon entry are *approximate*, as the dates change slightly each year.

New Moon (or solar eclipse) in Aries ♈

(Between late March and late April)

◗ 1. Take action

The New Moon in Aries marks the start of the New Moon cycle, since Aries is the first sign of the zodiac. The time for dreaming is over and the time to take action has come. You have a clean slate when it comes to making your New Moon wishes: if you've been lax about doing them, this is the time to get back on board.

◗ 2. Make a 12-month plan

This a wonderful time to make a plan for the year ahead. If you're attached, do one plan for yourself and another for you and your partner as a couple. Doing one for work won't hurt either.

Aries energy is really impulsive, so you might think it's too high energetically right now to make plans, but with a bit of discipline, anything is possible. The fiery, enthusiastic Aries energy is great for infusing your plans with drive and determination.

◗ 3. Be courageous

If you've been too timid and need courage to move forwards with whatever you're facing, include that in your wish list. Aries is connected to brave Mars, and the energies around the Aries New Moon reflect this. Decide that you can be bolder in life – and then work on it. Aries isn't so much bold as willing to just bowl into anything and everything, without being overly cautious about the results. If you could use a bit more of this impetuousness in your life, now is the time to incorporate it.

◗ 4. Have some fun!

Are you having enough fun? Being spontaneous often enough? Think about it and if the answer is 'no', then determine that over the coming weeks, you'll make more time for fun. Aries is the child of the zodiac and now is a good time to remind yourself to connect with your inner child.

◗ 5. Focus on you

This is also a time for some focus on yourself and what you need – where you're going and so on. If you give yourself, your wardrobe and your website just one makeover a year, do it now. Aries is traditionally the 'starting' sign, not least because it's the child of the zodiac: It's filled with vim and vigour as it prepares to bust out of the starting gate, and it's not going to worry about going too fast. It just 'does'. Action stations!

New Moon (or solar eclipse) in Taurus ♉

(Between late April and late May)

◗ 1. Make a financial plan

One of the most obvious, and perhaps helpful, things to do at the time of the New Moon in Taurus is to take a long hard look at your financial situation. Cash, property and possessions are all in focus at this time of the year. Money is really *not* a dirty word, unless you make it one, so have a think about where you stand financially now, versus where you'd like to be by the end of the year. Can you increase the amount of money that you set aside as savings each week?

◗ 2. Love yourself

One of the big issues to work on around this time is your self-worth. Think about what you value in yourself and what you value at large. If you don't value yourself, it stands to reason that other people are unlikely to do so either. Make a list of the top five things you value most. Are you living your life in a way that allows you to focus on these things? If not, what can you do about it? Tip: the answer isn't 'nothing'.

◗ 3. Be sensual

This is also a wonderful time to relax, if you can. Taurus may be a charging bull at times but the energy equally relates to the contented bull in the field, chewing the cud and enjoying the warm Sun on its back. Use the New Moon in Taurus to take a look around your life. Ask yourself: 'What would make my life better?' Can you find a way to allow some creature comforts into your life? The Taurus New Moon is also sensual, so use this month to titillate yourself and your senses. Have a massage. Eat well. Sleep late. Taurus is about feeling good in your body. It's about delicious physical pleasures and sensations, including taste, touch and smell.

◗ 4. Character check

Are you being too stubborn or too lazy? These are very reasonable questions to ask once a year, and the New Moon in the often stubborn and lazy Taurus is a wonderful time to do it. Or perhaps you aren't being lazy *enough*? See point 3.

◗ 5. Persevere

The flip side of point 4 is that even though the Taurus energy can be a tad indolent (and remember, we all have Taurus in our chart somewhere), it's also patient and earthy. Whatever you're working on right now, be it in your personal or professional life, this New Moon comes as a sign to you to wind things down a little, and to move slowly and surely towards your goals. Perseverance is the name of the game this month. Be dependable, too.

New Moon (or solar eclipse) in Gemini ♊

(Between late May and late June)

◗ 1. Communicate

Think about how well you're communicating with the people who matter most to you. Gemini is the sign most concerned with this subject, and the New Moon in Gemini is a wonderful time to check in with yourself. For example, are you being honest about how you feel? Or are you whingeing and then wondering why your 'requests' don't get the response you'd like?

◗ 2. Meditate

Think about your mental state. If, like most people, you feel as if your brain is racing most of the time, then one of your New

Moon wishes this month could be around promising yourself more mental time out. As I explained earlier, meditation is one of the best ways to relax your brain. You can do it even in the middle of the busiest day.

◗ 3. Socialize

Ask yourself how well you're greasing the social wheels in your life. Gemini is a wonderfully flirtatious sign (and we all have Gemini somewhere in our chart). So how are you doing when you go to a party, for example, or when you come up against a gaggle of fellow school mums, or when you're at work and you've no choice but to socialize? This is a good time to brush up on your lighthearted small talk! Seriously. If it doesn't already come easily to you, life will be easier if you work on this.

◗ 4. See your siblings

Get together with your sister(s) or brother(s) or neighbour(s). This might sound a bit superficial but if you only do it once a year, when the Moon is new in Gemini, at least you'll stay in touch. If you haven't been on good terms with a sibling, now is the time to make some changes there. Start by doing that most Gemini of things and talking or writing to your sibling as a first step to sorting things out.

◗ 5. Read more

Reading is also strongly associated with Gemini so get your reading list on track. What are you really interested in? Are you pursuing it? It's easy to lose years of our lives to browsing the internet or watching TV. At least once a year, at the Gemini New Moon, draw up a reading list for yourself. Order the books, pile them up somewhere visible and then work your way through them. Your life will thank you.

New Moon (or solar eclipse) in Cancer ♋

(Between late June and late July)

◗ 1. Family time

Check in with your mum and dad. The Cancerian energy is all about home and family, and nothing matters more to Cancerians. If you haven't spent enough time with your nearest and dearest lately, get in touch with them (if you don't have family nearby, or at all, people who feel like family also count). In particular, if there's tension between you and your family, use this New Moon to resolve to sort that out. Life is too short!

◗ 2. Banish insecurity

Be honest with yourself about whether you're coming from a place of insecurity, fear or possessiveness – anywhere (or everywhere) in your life. Consider the symbol of the sign of Cancer – the crab. It's a little creature with a very hard shell that protects a soft and vulnerable inside. That's the Cancerian vibe, and we all have it – we're all self-protective. This month, ask yourself if you're being too hard because you're worried. Identify and drop a few barriers. You'll feel better for it. Also, check that you're not being too moody. Meditation will help with this.

◗ 3. Nurture

Get in touch with your caring and nurturing side. Cancerian energy is very warm and cosy: think of a lovely white-haired grandma who holds you close when you're upset, and whose cups of tea or hot chocolate make you feel so much better. There's more to the Cancerian energy than that, but it's a big part of it. Make a promise to look after yourself this month. And look after others too, especially kids.

◗ 4. Review your goals

Cancer is also one of the most dynamic and tenacious signs. Perhaps all that caring and nurturing leaves people more able to go out into the world and achieve. So this month, go back to your goals for the year. The Cancer New Moon happens about midway through the year, so think about where you are with what you were aiming for at the start of the year, and think about what needs tweaking now, to stay on course (or to get back on course).

◗ 5. Bathe

One of the best things to do on a Cancerian New Moon is to have a lovely warm or hot bath, preferably by nontoxic candlelight (although please be aware of the health risks posed by many indoor candles). It's said that being in a warm bath recreates the conditions in the womb – no wonder it's so appealing to so many. Personally, I have some of my best ideas in the bath. Cancer is a Water sign, so doing anything connected with water now is good. If you're lucky enough to live near a pool, river, creek, ocean or sea, jump on in. Unwind with a watery theme. Brilliance often follows unwinding.

New Moon (or solar eclipse) in Leo ♌

(Between late July and late August)

◗ 1. Show off

The Leo New Moon is a time to celebrate life. And we all get to enjoy it, no matter what our sign. The Leo energy is generous, fun, magnanimous, and even a tad showy-offy. But guess what, we all have Leo in our chart somewhere, and this month, that part of your chart is being triggered. As Oprah Winfrey says, 'The more we praise and celebrate our lives, the more we have to praise and celebrate.' This is also a great time to take a holiday, so dream up your next getaway.

◗ 2. Flirt!

The Leo energy is also about the fun of flirtation and you're never too old for that! On the days after the New Moon in Leo, there's a good chance you'll feel a good buzz in the air. Whether you're with your beloved and seeking a few thrills or single and ready to mingle, bring sexy back. Enjoy a romantic evening: wine and dine someone; if you're single, wine and dine a friend, just for the pure fun of it.

◗ 3. Be creative

Too many people completely neglect their creativity. We all have a creative streak. For some of us, it comes out in art. For others, in the kitchen or doing crafts, or dreaming up wonderful holiday itineraries, or even creating mind-blowing spreadsheets. Whatever creativity means to you, now is the time to get back in touch with that part of you. Doing this once a year, at the time of the Leo New Moon, means it never gets to lie dormant for too long. Adults are so often serious. The Leo New Moon brings a chance to lighten up.

◗ 4. Love thyself

Pay something forward. Be giving. Open your heart. Leos get a lot of stick for boasting about themselves, but do you know what I say? Good on them. One of the most important things we can do for our wellbeing is to love ourselves. Use the power of this month's New Moon to get back in touch with what's so great about you. This doesn't have to be about arrogance. It's about self-love, and love is never arrogant. Work on your confidence and your leadership skills.

◗ 5. Spoil thyself

And then spoil someone you love. Indulge. Live a little! Leo is represented by the bright, hot Sun. When the New Moon is in Leo, it's time to walk your walk, talk your talk, shake your shimmy and generally remember that you're a hot little number with a lot to offer the world. There are no prizes for hiding your light under a bushel, right?

New Moon (or solar eclipse) in Virgo ♍

(Between late August and late September)

◗ 1. Take an inventory

Pay attention to the details. Take an inventory of your life. Work out what's working and what isn't. Virgo has a reputation for being picky – too right! The image for the sign of Virgo recalls the people who once used their powers of discernment literally to sort the wheat from the chaff – back in the days of people-skilled agriculture. So use the energies this month to think about where in your life you need to make changes. Pay particular attention to your daily routines.

◗ 2. Be of service

If you're on the spiritual path, you'll have heard teachers reminding us all that the best work is when we're of service to others. Virgo is all about being of service, so use this month to consider whether you're being of service to others. Think about what's going on at work, especially. How can you help other people? Service with a smile will attract karmic Brownie points. Easing a colleague's workload, or offering to pick up someone else's kid after school… It's the little things.

◗ 3. Be healthy

Virgo has a strong holistic health theme. The New Moon in this sign is a wonderful time to think about your diet and your daily habits. Much has been written about the importance of morning and evening routines, so how do yours look? Virgo is a fine habit-former, so start some beneficial new routines this month – be it morning or evening yoga, daily meditations, nutrient-packed breakfast smoothies, earlier nights or whatever – and see how long you can keep them going.

◗ 4. Avoid nitpicking

Are you being too critical? Use the New Moon in undeniably picky Virgo to assess this. Love and criticism, for example, don't go together so make sure you haven't allowed yourself to get into the habit of finding flaws in the people you love. Don't do it to yourself either! Doing your best is one thing, but perfectionism is another. Don't be too hard on yourself. Do as you'd be done by – a very Virgo way to be.

◗ 5. Get organized

Virgo is like the part of us that's 'together'. In other words, the part that's organized and punctual. Catch up with paying bills, filing paperwork and tidying up when the New Moon is in Virgo.

New Moon (or solar eclipse) in Libra ♎

(Between late September and late October)

◗ 1. Really relate

How well do you relate to others? Libra is the sign of partnership so use this month to ask yourself how well you're getting on with the important people in your life, and whether a little harmonization and negotiation would serve you better. Libra is all about harmony and cooperation, so bring these back into your life if they've been missing. The energy of Libra is about give and take, but more about give. It's *you* rather than *me*. How are you doing when it comes to being a friend, a lover, a partner, a coworker or even an ex?

◗ 2. Partner up

Partnerships in particular get special attention at this New Moon. If your marriage or your business partnership need work, issues may well arise now – all the better for you to sort them out. Libra is very social and diplomatic, so bring those qualities to the fore now as the New Moon is in this lovely and charming sign.

◗ 3. Negotiate

The New Moon in Libra is a wonderful time to negotiate or renegotiate anything you're not too happy with. Libra loves to bring things into balance. Find points of accord. Make 'I agree' your motto for a day and see what happens.

◗ 4. Look gorgeous

Libra is also refined and beautiful. So if you need to balance things out in order to live a more beautiful and refined life, take action this month while you have the Libra New Moon energy backing you up. I don't mean to sound superficial, but the image we present to the world says a lot about us. Libra is about beauty – are you feeling as good as you can about yourself? How about art – do you have some of that in your life to enrich it aesthetically? If not, get some!

◗ 5. Regain your identity

Consider whether you're exhibiting codependency, i.e. relying too much on someone else for your sense of wellbeing. Libra is all about partnerships but sometimes the 'togetherness' thing can go too far. Have you lost your sense of identity in someone else? If so, this is the ideal time to do something about it.

New Moon (or solar eclipse) in Scorpio ♏

(Between late October and late November)

◗ 1. Get sexy

The energy of the New Moon in Scorpio is very sexy. That's because Scorpio is the sign that isn't afraid of its dark side, or of showing itself in an unguarded moment. And of course sex works best when people forget themselves and stop worrying about how they look. So many of us grew up being told that sex is in some ways dirty, but Scorpio is the sign that will get down and dirty, and smile lasciviously as it goes. And we all have Scorpio energy.

◗ 2. Invest wisely

Financial partnerships also come under the New Moon in Scorpio. In other words, where your money meets, or works with, someone else's. Some obvious scenarios include your salary, credit cards and debts as well as mortgages, wills and inheritances. If you want to start or finish a financial partnership, now is a good time for it (although the *Full* Moon in Scorpio is arguably better for finishing it off).

◗ 3. Make inner peace

Possessiveness and jealousy are also very much the Scorpio energy. Are you going through anything that involves such feelings? A power struggle with someone, say? This relates back to the Dark Side of Scorpio. Don't reject this part of yourself; rather, use the New Moon in Scorpio energy coming through right now to make peace with it. The less you repress it, the less trouble it will cause you. This doesn't give you carte blanche to turn into a raging jealous beast, though! Rather, it means acknowledging that you have these feelings, and dealing with them in a way that's safe for all involved.

◗ 4. B-r-e-a-t-h-e

With all this Scorpio intensity, you won't be surprised to hear that the New Moon in Scorpio is a really good time to deepen your relationships, sexual or otherwise. Just don't let your attraction to someone become too obsessive. A bit of an obsession with someone or something can be fun, but it can also go too far. Look at your actions, and if you know you're being compulsive, then deal with it kindly. Commitments made at the New Moon in Scorpio usually have serious staying power.

◗ 5. Drop grudges

This is also the time to ditch emotional baggage and drop grudges. These are toxic and destructive, and the New Moon in Scorpio is the time to face up to them for what they are. Suspicions, guilt and thoughts of revenge are also somewhat easier to deal with at this time. Sort them out. Life is too short. And karma is too much of a drag. Oh yes, karma is also Scorpionic. Remember, the New Moon is 'turning the corner' time. Work on these parts of yourself once a year.

New Moon (or solar eclipse) in Sagittarius ♐

(Between late November and late December)

◗ 1. Get away

Travel, and whatever else represents freedom to you – these are two of the most fun things you can expect to come up now. If you're feeling hemmed in by life and need to get away from it all, use the power of the New Moon in the freedom-loving and wandering sign of Sagittarius either to make a travel booking or actually take off. Sagittarius is the sign that knows that things can always get better, and sometimes we just need a new perspective to see how blessed our lives are.

◗ 2. Study

Study is also a worthwhile pursuit this month. Sometimes studying seems like a drag, but the truth is that it brings freedom because it opens us up to more work opportunities which, in turn, can bring more cash and money and thus more freedom, at least to some degree.

◗ 3. Search for meaning

The Great Cosmic Quest also comes into view this month. In other words, it's time to search life for some meaning. How are you doing with that? Sagittarius is the keeper of life philosophies. The New Moon in this sign is a good time to check that you're not being narrow-minded.

◗ 4. Laugh

Having fun and taking risks are both under the remit of the New Moon in Sagittarius. If life has become a tad staid, ask yourself if you're doing enough of either. I'm not suggesting you do a high-wire walk between the Petronas Towers, but use the power of the New Moon in Sagittarius to introduce some kind of 'spin of the wheel of fortune' into your life. Excess isn't only extra-possible now, it's positively encouraged. On the other side of things, know that Sagittarius touches on legal issues. The Sagittarius New Moon brings new energy into any ongoing battles.

◗ 5. Be grateful

Know that you're blessed! Sagittarius is a sign that can bring us perspective. If you've been moaning or focusing on the negative, then use this time to turn that around. As my teacher in India says, 'The secret of life is to know that you're blessed, and to live your life within that knowing.'

New Moon (or solar eclipse) in Capricorn ♑

(Between late December and late January)

◗ 1. Plan

It might be the end of the year but Capricorn is all about planning. Use this time to have a think about what you want to achieve *next* year. Yes, this book is all about planning and writing things down, because these are the main secrets to successful manifesting! Capricorn knows that you have to go slow and steady towards your goals, so check in and see how you're doing with yours.

◗ 2. Be ambitious

This is also a time to be very ambitious – very definite in your goals. Think about what you want to be known for. Capricorn is no slouch: it knows that hard work is the way to long-term goal achievement. Have you been thinking too rigidly? Use the New Moon in Capricorn to promise yourself you'll replace rigid thinking with mature, tempered, strategic thinking. If you crave social status or recognition for what you do, this New Moon is the time to work on advancing yours, whatever that means to you. (No judgement.)

◗ 3. Be kind

One thing to be aware of at this time is that the Capricorn energy (which liaises with the serious planet Saturn) can be rather cold. Use the season of goodwill around you now, and the New Moon in Capricorn energy, to show someone how much they mean to you. Make promises you intend to keep. Show someone you're in it for the long haul.

◗ 4. Cede control

Avoid being controlling, though. Capricorn is a very tough sign in many ways. And like every other sign, we all have it in our chart somewhere. If you know you have a tendency to be unbending, harness the Capricorn New Moon and make a plan for how to change that. No one likes to be controlled.

◗ 5. Establish traditions

Establishing a new tradition at this time of the year is a wonderful thing to do, whether it's related to Christmas or not. Thinking about your reputation, and working on it, is also worth doing now too. Thanking your boss, or your employees, is also recommended. These might feel like natural things to do at the end of the year, but the New Moon in Capricorn works so well with them, they're doubly worth doing.

New Moon (or solar eclipse) in Aquarius ♒

(Between late January and late February)
Note that the New Moon in Aquarius heralds Chinese New Year.

◗ 1. Detach

Release and let go of attachment at this New Moon (*see Part III*). Aquarius is the most detached sign of all. People get confused about Aquarius because although it's the Water Bearer, it's an Air sign and as such it tends to live a lot inside its own head. This has its drawbacks of course, but overall, the place where we have Aquarius in our chart is where we can be pragmatic, as opposed to overly emotional and too led by feelings only. Sometimes logic is called for.

◗ 2. Be true

Use the New Moon in Aquarius to ask yourself if you're giving yourself the space to be your true, own unique self. Aquarius is the sign that doesn't care about convention as much as the rest of us. It actually makes sense that Valentine's Day falls in the Aquarius period, since people fall in love when they see someone's real self, weird bits and all.

◗ 3. Be inventive

If you're feeling stumped by someone or something, harness the New Moon in Aquarius to come up with a new idea or invention or solution. The Aquarius energy is all about looking forwards to the future and what's next. It's a fashion-forward sign that also rules technology and progress. If you've become stuck in a rut, this is the time of year to acknowledge that and make some changes. Make like the Aquarius energy and care less about society's norms. (Within reason, mind – do no harm!)

◗ 4. Be charitable

If you only make one charitable donation a year, make it when the New Moon in Aquarius is taking place. Aquarius is an energy that wants to work for the betterment of the human race and this is the time for all of us to do our bit.

◗ 5. Connect

Be sociable this month too. Aquarius is a funny sign in that it's almost better at relating to large groups of people than it is one on one. That's why it's such a humanitarian sign. So when the New Moon in Aquarius takes place, it's a great time to check in with your friends and social circles. Aquarius has a real sense of people getting together for a common ideal, so seek out your tribe.

New Moon (or solar eclipse) in Pisces ♓

(Between late February and late March)

◗ 1. Dream…

Ah, the lovely dreamy place that's Pisces! This is the home of dreams, mystical matters and compassion. Think about what you're thinking about. Think about what you're dreaming about. Are you using your imagination for good – that means to attract all that you want? This is the New Moon when you can work on releasing fear.

◗ 2. Face your fears

The New Moon in Pisces is also about secrets, and sometimes about lies. It's about the things we don't want to admit to ourselves or anyone else. Take an inventory of your fears at the time of this New Moon and you could find yourself liberating yourself of some of your fears. These spineless little critters often run in the opposite direction when they're confronted head on, and now is the time to do that.

◗ 3. Get cosmic!

Because of all the mystical energy around when the Pisces energy is so strong, it's a wonderful time to work on your intuitive skills. Make a note of your hunches and see what transpires. Play around with Tarot or Archangel cards and test your results.

◗ 4. Heal

If you're suffering emotionally or spiritually, note that there's extra easy access to healing energies when the New Moon in Pisces takes place. The sign is strongly associated with Neptune, a planet that has the power to take ethereal shreds of an idea and turn them into daydreams – and as we all know, daydreams can come true, thanks to the Law of Attraction. If you need spiritual healing, seek out a healer. Ask friends for a recommendation. Also make a list of what 'being healed' would entail for you, and see it happening – then tick things off as they come to pass.

◗ 5. Surrender

Note that Pisces is about dreams, so write down your dreams this month. What do you want? What are your fantasies, sexual or otherwise? Seek bliss. Surrender to the Universe and trust that what you need is what's happening. Practising yoga and other spiritual activities is highly recommended around the time of the Pisces New Moon (and beyond). This is the time to access your higher self: the part of you that knows you're connected to all life everywhere.

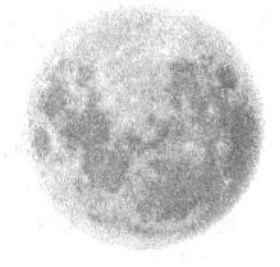

CHAPTER 5

Predict Your Future with the New Moon

One of the things people love about astrology is that it can help you to predict the future. And it's possible to do this with the New Moon too, just by looking at which *House* the New Moon falls in (your astrological birth chart is organized into 12 sections, each of which is known as a House. And each of the 12 Houses rules a different part of your life). In fact, the New Moon can be used as an *amazing* life guide and predictor. It can give you an idea of:

- What to expect in the coming month.
- Where your focus can, will, and even should be for the month ahead.
- Where it will be easier for you to wipe the slate clean and start again.
- What kinds of things you should be doing in the coming four weeks.
- The themes of the coming four weeks.

Star signs/rising signs and Houses

You'll need to know your star sign (aka your zodiac sign) and/or your rising sign in order to make predictions with the New Moon, so before we go any further, let's just make sure you do.

Look for your birth date in the table of star signs below. Note that if you were born on or near one of the changeover dates shown, you do need to double-check your sign, as the Sun moves into the different signs with a variation of a couple of days from year to year. You can do that at my site (moonologybook.com/freechart).

Star sign		Birth date
♈	Aries	March 21–April 19
♉	Taurus	April 20–May 20
♊	Gemini	May 21–June 20
♋	Cancer	June 21–July 22
♌	Leo	July 23–August 22
♍	Virgo	August 23–September 22
♎	Libra	September 23–October 22
♏	Scorpio	October 23–November 21
♐	Sagittarius	November 22–December 21
♑	Capricorn	December 22–January 19
♒	Aquarius	January 20–February 18
♓	Pisces	February 19–March 20

If you're content to move ahead with only your star sign, that's fine. You can still follow the New Moon each month and get reasonably precise predictions regarding what to expect in the four weeks following the New Moon. *However, using your rising sign will give you a more accurate reading.*

Your rising sign is the *most personal point* on your horoscope chart because it's calculated using your time, date and place of birth. In other words, someone born at the exact same moment as you on the other side of the world (or even just a few miles away) won't have the same rising sign details as you.

Find your rising sign

To find your rising sign, aka your ascendant, go to moonmessages.com/freechart and cast your chart for free. If you don't know your time of birth, ask your family or check your birth certificate. If you were born in a hospital, you can try calling them as they sometimes have records.

If neither approach works and you're determined to find out your time of birth, there are two further methods you can try. Firstly, you can get muscle tested. This is when a kinesiologist asks your body what time you were born, working on the theory that our bodies know everything. You can also see what's called a rectification astrologer – someone who will reverse engineer the time by looking at the timing of major events in your life (for example, when you graduated from school, met your partner, married, had a child, etc.). Ideally you'd see a kinesiologist and a rectification astrologer, and the times would independently line up.

Find the House the New Moon is in

Now you have both your star and rising signs, you're almost ready to discover what the New Moon (and indeed the Full Moon,

Quarter Moon and Daily Moon) means for you personally. But first you'll need to use the table on pages 84–85 to check which House the New Moon is triggering for you personally, from month to month.

Here are a few samples, so you can see how the table works:

- If you're Taurus or Taurus rising, the New Moon in Scorpio is in your 7th House
- If you're Pisces or Pisces rising, the New Moon in Aquarius is in your 12th House
- If you're Sagittarius or Sagittarius rising, the New Moon in Libra is in your 11th House

A guide to the New Moon in each House

What follows is a guide for you to use at every New Moon from now to forever. To do that, first find out which *sign* the New Moon is in. You can find that on the home page of my site, yasminboland.com. Then turn to the table on pages 84–85, find your star sign or rising sign in the left column and scan across to the column of the New Moon to discover which *House* it's is in for you. *Note that this grid can also be used to find out which House the Full Moon, Daily Moon or any other Moon is in for you.*

In the rest of this chapter I take your through each New Moon and House to help you understand what it's likely to portend:

- The issues that each New Moon is likely to raise for you.
- What to do and expect at each New Moon and in the four weeks that follow.
- My suggestions for what to wish for at each New Moon.
- My suggestions for what to visualize at each New Moon.

- The idea to keep in mind at each New Moon, and in the four weeks that follow.
- The main messages of each New Moon.
- A way to boost your regular meditation practice.
- The ritual to perform at each New Moon.
- The top 3 affirmations to say at each New Moon.

Within the guide you'll also find what I call cosmic extras. That's the information about:

- Essential oils: I explain which ones are best to use at each New Moon.
- The numerological energy of each New Moon: the numbers to look out for.
- Mantras: I've listed the best ones to chant at New Moon and in the four weeks that follow. These help you connect with the energy of the Moon and to boost your manifesting practice.
- Goddesses and Archangels: learn which ones guide each New Moon.
- The Universal Laws: At each New Moon, and in the four weeks that follow, contemplate one of these laws.
- The Heavenly Rays: Discover which ray is associated with each New Moon, and what to do with it.

So without further ado, let's go. Please note that I can personalize the following information for you every month. Find out more at mainlymoonologymembership.com.

Your star sign or rising sign	The Moon in Aries is in your...	The Moon in Taurus is in your...	The Moon in Gemini is in your...	The Moon in Cancer is in your...	The Moon in Leo is in your...
Aries or Aries rising	1st House	2nd House	3rd House	4th House	5th House
Taurus or Taurus rising	12th House	1st House	2nd House	3rd House	4th House
Gemini or Gemini rising	11th House	12th House	1st House	2nd House	3rd House
Cancer or Cancer rising	10th House	11th House	12th House	1st House	2nd House
Leo or Leo rising	9th House	10th House	11th House	12th House	1st House
Virgo or Virgo rising	8th House	9th House	10th House	11th House	12th House
Libra or Libra rising	7th House	8th House	9th House	10th House	11th House
Scorpio or Scorpio rising	6th House	7th House	8th House	9th House	10th House
Sagittarius or Sagittarius rising	5th House	6th House	7th House	8th House	9th House
Capricorn or Capricorn rising	4th House	5th House	6th House	7th House	8th House
Aquarius or Aquarius rising	3rd House	4th House	5th House	6th House	7th House
Pisces or Pisces rising	2nd House	3rd House	4th House	5th House	6th House

The Moon in Virgo is in your...	The Moon in Libra is in your...	The Moon in Scorpio is in your...	The Moon in Sagittarius is in your...	The Moon in Capricorn is in your...	The Moon in Aquarius is in your...	The Moon in Pisces is in your...
6th House	7th House	8th House	9th House	10th House	11th House	12th House
5th House	6th House	7th House	8th House	9th House	10th House	11th House
4th House	5th House	6th House	7th House	8th House	9th House	10th House
3rd House	4th House	5th House	6th House	7th House	8th House	9th House
2nd House	3rd House	4th House	5th House	6th House	7th House	8th House
1st House	2nd House	3rd House	4th House	5th House	6th House	7th House
12th House	1st House	2nd House	3rd House	4th House	5th House	6th House
11th House	12th House	1st House	2nd House	3rd House	4th House	5th House
10th House	11th House	12th House	1st House	2nd House	3rd House	4th House
9th House	10th House	11th House	12th House	1st House	2nd House	3rd House
8th House	9th House	10th House	11th House	12th House	1st House	2nd House
7th House	8th House	9th House	10th House	11th House	12th House	1st House

New Moon (or solar eclipse) in your 1st House

(Also known as your Image Zone)

◗ It's all about...

The image you're presenting to the world.

◗ What to expect

The chance to change the way that someone – or the world – sees you.

◗ What to wish for

Courage, a new beginning, a better self-image and self-direction.

◗ What to visualize

Yourself, looking exactly as you'd like to.

◗ Idea to keep in mind

This is the start of my new 12-month cycle and I'm beginning as I mean to continue.

◗ Messages

This New Moon is one of the most exciting because it's all about the ever-changing and wonderful *you!* It's a time for self-improvement and self-development. Your personal appearance should be a priority this month – you're allowed to be a bit vain.

Get yourself into the kind of shape you've been dreaming of and take a closer look at the image you're presenting. This may sound superficial but pride in your appearance and an awareness of the message it sends out are a key to success. You can dress any way you want to, but give it some thought this month.

This New Moon cycle also offers your annual chance to clear out your wardrobe, get a drop-dead gorgeous new haircut, have some up-to-date business cards made or revamp your website. Basically, it's all about the way you present yourself to the world.

Your popularity is high this month, so accept the invitations coming your way and revel in the attention. This is also one of the best times of the year for starting all kinds of new projects.

You're in focus and in the spotlight this month. Make it your selfie month. If you need to work on your self-confidence in relation to your appearance, the New Moon will support you.

◗ Meditation booster

Recite the following sentence to yourself before you start your regular meditation: *'I allow myself to evolve and change.'*

◗ Ritual

Do the following just after making your New Moon wishes: Stand in front of a mirror, blow your reflection a loving kiss and say: 'I love you!'

◗ Things to do

- Surprise friends with the 'new you'.
- Throw out all your old make-up and start again.
- This is a great time to get married or meet someone new.
- It's also a good time to move home.
- Splurge on something in a vibrant colour.
- Have a facial.
- Get your sight checked.

◗ Top 3 affirmations

Repeat one or all three daily during this New Moon, and in the coming four weeks:

1. 'Today is the first day of the rest of my life!'
2. 'I take pride in my appearance.'
3. 'I am brave!'

◗ Essential oil

As you begin your new journey, angelica seed will ease any doubts and increase self-awareness and positivity. Use angelica seed at this New Moon and for the coming four weeks – in your bath, in a burner or on your body.

◗ Numerological energy

The number this month is 1, which means this is a time to think about yourself a little more than usual. What are your dreams, aims and goals? Get centred. Be very aware that you're at the start of your new 12-month New Moon cycle. Forget about the past and focus on what you want for yourself in the present, and what you wish to create for yourself in the future.

◗ Mantra

Use the mantra *Ram* this month. Chant it out loud or silently every day: while you're in the shower, before or after meditating, or at any other time that feels right to you.

◗ Guiding Archangel

Ariel is the Archangel known as the Angelic Ambassador of Divine Magic and Miraculous Manifestation. Ariel reminds us that anything is possible if we approach life with the innocence of a child. Doing so can work wonders. To connect with Archangel Ariel, simply say the name Ariel and ask for help:

> *'Dearest Archangel Ariel, please be with me this month as I start this important new cycle in my*

life. With your help and guidance, I can reach my full potential in all areas of my life. Thank you.'

◗ Guiding Goddess

Athena is a powerful Goddess who can help you as you start new projects. She's the Warrior Goddess and Protector. Call upon her for any courage you may need: she has no fear. To connect with Athena, simply say her name and ask for help.

◗ Universal Law

This month's law is the Law of Divine Oneness, which states that we're all connected to all life everywhere; everything we think, do and say has a knock-on effect on us and on the people – and indeed on the world and Universe – around us.

◗ Heavenly Ray

This month's ray is the 1st ray, which is governed by Ascended Master El Morya and overseen by the Manu Allah Gobi. The ray is red, so as you meditate this month, bring the colour red to mind. The 1st ray will anchor everything you need as you start your new cycle: ask for courage, confidence, inner power, bravery, passion, driving force and enthusiasm. Ask that your will integrates with the will and divine plan of the Creator.

New Moon (or solar eclipse) in your 2nd House

(Also known as your Cash, Property and Values Zone)

◗ It's all about…

Your cash and property, and your talents and assets.

◗ What to expect

Money and possessions will be in focus this month.

◗ What to wish for

Financial abundance, increased self-esteem, that 'thing' you really want.

◗ What to visualize

See yourself in your ideal home, happy with loved ones.

◗ Idea to keep in mind

Is my life stable and if not, what steps will help me make it so?

◗ Messages

This New Moon can help you start over financially. It's a time to remember your own fabulousness and magnificence. It gives you a special chance to take a look at your assets – and I'm not just talking about the ones in the bank. It's deeper than that. What do you have to offer the world? Value yourself and others will follow suit. It also asks you to take a look at and work on your self-worth and self-esteem. Love thyself. There's nothing wrong and everything right about doing this.

Income, finances and budgets all figure now. How can you find some stability in these areas? The New Moon supports you as you work on these parts of your life. Believing in yourself is a first step. The higher you rate yourself, the higher others will rate you. I'm not talking about bragging, here: more deep-down self-belief. Make financial management a priority this month. Think about what you really value and about what you have to offer the world.

◗ Meditation booster

Recite the following sentence before you start your regular meditation: 'I believe in myself and what I have to offer the world.'

◗ Ritual

Just after making your New Moon wishes, write down the amount of money you'd like to receive.

◗ Things to do

- Start a savings account.
- Pay your bills, taxes, debts, etc.
- Hire an accountant, if it's all too much.
- Showcase your talents.
- Get a neck and shoulder massage.
- Invest in an expensive neck cream.
- Make love in the countryside.

◗ Top 3 affirmations

Repeat one or all three daily during this New Moon, and in the coming four weeks:

1. 'I am happy, healthy, wealthy and wise!'
2. 'Thank you, Universe – all my needs are provided for!'
3. 'I'm worth it!'

◗ Essential oil

A wonderful oil for calming any fears you may have around money is ylang-ylang. It's a very relaxing oil – just what you need if you have money worries. Breathe in deeply, and remember that money is energy and responds to our emotions.

◗ Numerological energy

This month's number is 2, which reminds you to work on loving yourself – if you've been comparing yourself to other people, it's time to stop that. Get in touch with your feminine side, whether you're male or female.

◗ Mantra

Use the mantra *Lam* this month. Chant it out loud or silently every day: while you're in the shower, before or after meditating, or at any other time that feels right to you.

◗ Guiding Archangel

Like all Archangels, Chamuel can help with anything you ask for assistance with, but his 'special subjects' include helping humans in our lifelong quests for relationships, friendships, the right job and inner peace. To connect with Archangel Chamuel, simply say his name and ask for help:

'Dearest Archangel Chamuel, please be with me this month as I find my way. With your help and guidance, I can reach my full potential in all areas of my life. Thank you.'

◗ Guiding Goddess

Abundantia was a divine personification of abundance and prosperity in the religion of ancient Rome. She's most often depicted holding a cornucopia that overflows with bounty – it pours forth abundance, good luck, good fortune, success and endless opportunities. Her name means 'plenty' or 'overflowing with riches'. She's most certainly the go-to prosperity Goddess if you have any financial issues.

◗ Universal Law

This month the law to reflect on is the Law of Vibration, which states that everything in the known Universe vibrates. It moves and travels in circular patterns. Similarly, our thoughts, words, feelings and desires are all vibration too. Raising our vibrations through singing, dancing, chanting, beautiful music or meditation will help us to align with the Universe.

◗ Heavenly Ray

The 2nd ray, which is blue, is governed by Master Joshua and overseen by the Christ Lord Maitreya. It anchors Source wisdom and is known to help us mere mortals with our spiritual development. If working on your spiritual development is something you'd like to do, bring the colour blue to mind regularly during your meditation this month.

New Moon (or solar eclipse) in your 3rd House

(Also known as your Communications Zone)

◗ It's all about...

Communicating – listening and talking – and spending time with your siblings.

◗ What to expect

A very busy month!

◗ What to wish for

The ability to express yourself clearly.

◗ What to visualize

Hugging someone, knowing that you've made your point lovingly.

◗ Idea to keep in mind

Are you speaking your truth, and if not, why are you covering it up? Explore this idea this month and be rigorously honest with yourself and others (without being cruel, of course).

◗ Messages

It's time to brush up on your powers of communication. How well are you doing at getting your message across? If you want something that someone else is in a position to give you, do you feel confident about asking for it (whether during a conversation or in an email)?

It's so important to express yourself and your desires clearly, and not to expect others to know you well enough to second-guess you. This New Moon offers the chance to start again when it comes to written and spoken communications. It can also signal the start of a very busy time with lots of quick, short trips and/or more time spent with brothers and sisters.

◗ Meditation booster

Recite the following sentence before you start your regular meditation: 'I read, listen and learn; and I breathe deeply when I'm stressed.'

◗ Ritual

Chant to boost your Throat chakra.

◗ Things to do

- Take a public speaking course.
- Read those books you've got stacked up.

- Take a short trip.
- Hang out with your sister or brother.
- Study a foreign language.
- Really listen to others.
- Write those letters you've been putting off.

◗ Top 3 affirmations

Repeat one or all three daily during this New Moon, and in the coming four weeks.

1. 'I am expressing myself clearly, kindly and fearlessly.'
2. 'I listen as much as I speak.'
3. 'My relationship with my sibling/neighbour gets better.'

◗ Essential oil

Bergamot is very useful to oil the wheels of communication. Use it at this New Moon and for the coming four weeks – in your bath, in a burner or on your body.

◗ Numerological energy

Work on having some fun with this month's number – 3 – which is about creativity and expression. The energy of this number is about the way we enjoy life when we're fully self-expressed and it just flows.

◗ Mantra

Use the mantra *Hum* this month. Chant it out loud or silently every day: while you're in the shower, before or after meditating, or at any other time that feels right to you.

Guiding Archangel

Archangel Zadkiel is the Archangel of compassion and forgiveness that comes from the heart. He's also the Archangel of memory. To connect with Archangel Zadkiel, simply light a candle, say the name Zadkiel, and ask for help:

'Dearest Archangel Zadkiel, please be with me this month as I express myself openly and honestly with everyone. With your help and guidance, I can reach my full potential when it comes to communicating. Thank you.'

You can also ask Zadkiel for help regarding your siblings or neighbours, if you need it.

Guiding Goddess

Saraswati is the Hindu Goddess of Intelligence and Divine Feminine Wisdom. She's also the Goddess who gave language to the world. So whether you're writing something or talking or presenting, ask Saraswati for help. When this part of your chart is triggered, it's time for you to think about how well you're getting your message across. Personally and professionally. To connect with Saraswati, simply say her name and ask for help.

Universal Law

The Law of Action is in focus this month. What happens if you have lots of hopes and dreams but you do nothing? Most likely, nothing. The Universal Law of Action must be activated in order for us to manifest the life we're dreaming of here on Earth. Are you taking action? What can you do to move closer to your dreams?

Heavenly Ray

The yellow 3rd ray is governed by Master Serapis Bey and overseen by Saint Germain. It anchors the power to manifest through the power of the mind, and brings clear-mindedness. Surrounding yourself with yellow during this cycle will remind you to allow light into your life, in the form of knowledge that comes in through an open mind.

New Moon (or solar eclipse) in your 4th House

(Also known as your Home and Family Zone)

◗ It's all about...

Home and family, where you come from, where home is, what family means.

◗ What to expect

Issues related to home and family may well come to the fore.

◗ What to wish for

A happy and healthy home life.

◗ What to visualize

A perfect day out, or in, with your family, or with people who feel like family.

◗ Idea to keep in mind

Your home; where you come from and where you belong.

◗ Messages

What does 'home' mean to you? Whatever your answer, it gives you a strong hint about the parts of your life that are going to be in focus over the coming four weeks.

The New Moon in this part of your chart often signifies starting again as far as your home is concerned – it can herald a house move, someone moving in or out of your home, major decluttering, renovating or redecorating.

Families often come to the forefront when the Moon's new in this part of your chart – your mother and father especially could take up more of your time now.

◗ Meditation booster

Recite the following sentence before you start your meditations: 'I know where I belong.'

◗ Ritual

Draw a picture of your family (or people who feel like family). No drawing talent is needed: they can be stick figures. Then draw a large love heart around them. Send each person love, one by one.

◗ Things to do

- Have a garage sale.
- Hug your parents.
- Sort out your photo albums/digital photo files.
- Invite friends over.
- Renovate or redecorate so you're more comfortable at home.
- Sell your home and/or change location, or even country.
- Ask your grandparents about your family's history.

◗ Top 3 affirmations

Repeat one or all three daily during this New Moon, and in the coming four weeks.

1. 'I love my family and my family love me.'

2. 'I am safe and all is well' – Louise Hay's famous affirmation works well here.
3. 'I love my home!' (Remember, affirmations manifest. Feel the feeling of loving your home so you move towards it – even if you don't totally love your present home.)

◗ Essential oil

Patchouli is an uplifting aphrodisiac that positively impacts the spirit. It reduces depression and boosts the immune system. Put it in your burner and spice things up at home.

◗ Numerological energy

The number 4 is all about being organized, practical and productive. Think of it as the four pillars that hold up the world. It's about being disciplined, strong, reliable and stable.

◗ Mantra

Use the mantra *Om* this month. Chant it out loud or silently every day: while you're in the shower, before or after meditating, or at any other time that feels right to you.

◗ Guiding Archangel

Archangel Gabriel is strongly associated with family, pregnancy and child-rearing. He leads hopeful parents towards child conception. And once you have a child and you're learning about parenthood and the wonders and challenges that go with it, Archangel Gabriel helps all who ask. To connect with Archangel Gabriel, simply light a candle, say the name Gabriel, and ask for help:

> *'Dearest Archangel Gabriel, please be with me this month as I work on my personal life, and on my family relationships*

and [insert anything else here that applies]. With your help and guidance, I can reach my full potential. Thank you.'

You can also ask Gabriel for help regarding your home, if you need it.

◗ Guiding Goddess

Talk to Diana, Goddess of the Hunt and Witches, if you're chasing someone or something, if you want to forget about formality and just be free to be yourself and pursue your goals, if you need to be more independent or if you've been too clingy lately. She can also help you with your parenting skills or if you've been smothering friends or family with too much parental-style love lately. To connect with Diana, simply say her name and ask for help.

◗ Universal Law

The Law of Correspondence reminds us that our outer life is a reflection of our inner life. It's the 'As Above, So Below, As Within, So Without' principle. So our life, our world, our reality, is a mirror of what's going on inside us. If our outer reality is messy, unhappy or unsatisfying, that's a direct reflection of what's happening inside us.

◗ Heavenly Ray

The 4th ray is governed by Master Paul the Venetian and overseen by Saint Germain. Peace, tranquillity, balance and harmony are all out there in the ether and waiting to be anchored in by you. This ray is green, so focus on this colour in your meditations and ask Saint Germain for help. This ray can also bring forth creative artistic abilities and help you to express your soul urges creatively, revealing your own inner beauty. It's also a cleansing ray.

◗ New Moon (or solar eclipse) in your 5th House

(Also known as your Fun Zone)

◗ It's all about…

Creativity, kids and romance – maybe one, maybe all three.

◗ What to expect

Fun and laughter, time with kids, creative surges.

◗ What to wish for

To remember that life is a game.

◗ What to visualize

Having a good time with people you love.

◗ Idea to keep in mind

Life is as fun as we make it.

◗ Messages

The part of your chart being triggered relates to three main areas: creativity, children and sexy romance (as opposed to the more serious stuff).

Where creativity is concerned, if you're a bit of a closet artist, the next four weeks will give you an excellent chance to work on your skills.

Where sexy romance is concerned, budding new romances are possible now and old romances could feel brand new if you make the most of this month's New Moon and look for ways to inject more erotic fun.

And kids? Whether they're your own or someone else's, kids are usually a big issue when the Moon's new in the 5th House.

◗ Meditation booster

Recite the following sentence before you start your meditations: 'My inner child will have a ball this month.'

◗ Ritual

Laugh out loud for a good minute or two. Don't worry about feeling silly. Just do it!

◗ Things to do

- Take up belly dancing – it's erotic and physical, which sums up the 5th House.
- Make a toy for a child (your own or someone else's).
- Take a lover.
- Take your lover on an adventure.
- Write a short story or paint a picture – just get creative.
- Do something that typifies your idea of fun; throw a party.

◗ Top 3 affirmations

Repeat one or all three daily during this New Moon, and in the coming four weeks.

1. 'Life is sweet!'
2. 'I now release my inner child for some fun!'
3. 'I am a creative being and my juices are flowing.'

◗ Essential oil

Cinnamon is a lesser-known oil that's really useful for 5th House matters. For one thing, it's an aphrodisiac and this part of the chart has a very flirty feel to it. It controls blood sugars – in other words, if you've been going wild with your 5th House and having too much fun, it can regulate things for you. It's also known as one of the happy-making essential oils and this part of your chart is all about having fun.

◗ Numerological energy

The number 5 is all about being independent. It's always in motion and in need of change – much like a child. And of course, kids come under the 5th House. So embrace your kids or embrace your inner child this month.

◗ Mantra

Use the mantra *Vam* this month. Chant it out loud or silently every day: while you're in the shower, before or after meditating, or at any other time that feels right to you.

◗ Guiding Archangel

Archangel Raziel teaches people about esoteric information. He's the Archangel who can help us to understand deep spiritual symbolism, past lives, dream interpretation, sacred geometry and so on.

Think of the Tarot card The Sun and you'll get a sense of how Archangel Raziel and the 5th House work together, bringing light and understanding where there has been confusion or misunderstanding. To connect with Archangel Raziel, simply light a candle, say his name, and ask for help:

> *'Dearest Archangel Raziel, please be with me this month as I work on letting my light shine. With your help and guidance, I can reach my full potential. Thank you.'*

You can also ask Raziel for help if you need it regarding your actual home.

Guiding Goddess

Talk to Medusa, the Sun Goddess, if you're willing to see life as it really is, to be bold and to chase your dreams without worrying about who may or may not approve. Talk to Medusa if you're willing to shine your light out into the world without fear of treading on someone's toes. To connect with Medusa, simply say her name and ask for help.

Universal Law

This month's law is the Law of Cause and Effect. Accept that everything happens for a reason – there's a cause and an effect. To put it another way, nothing happens by chance. For every action (including our thoughts) there's a reaction or consequence. 'We reap what we sow'. What does this mean to you? Notice what happens this month and ask yourself 'why?'

Heavenly Ray

The orange 5th ray is governed by Master Hilarion and overseen by Saint Germain. This ray is connected with ascension and the spiritual growth process. It's also about the activation and evolution of the soul. It assists science but at a higher level. It also boosts the ability of the soul to integrate with 'what is' in our lives, here in the 3rd dimension.

New Moon (or solar eclipse) in your 6th House

(Also known as your Daily Work and Health Zone)

It's all about...

Your daily work and health routines.

What to expect

A chance to change your daily habits and/or your job description.

◗ What to wish for

The opportunity to help other people.

◗ What to visualize

See yourself adopting a very healthy new habit or continuing with an existing one.

◗ Idea to keep in mind

Healthy body, healthy mind. There really is a connection and as the 6th House of your chart is triggered, it's time to work on that connection. This is a once-a-year chance to really clean up your system and to reap the benefits of a cleaner, leaner life.

◗ Messages

The part of your chart being triggered is about the body, the mind and your wellbeing. If you haven't been looking after yourself, problems may come up now, trying to grab your attention about what needs to be done.

It's a perfect time to join the gym or take up exercise routines that you've let slip. It's also a great time to start again where health is concerned – to give up smoking or alter your diet, for example.

Also under the microscope are your daily work routines. Remember that a New Moon is about beginnings, so use this month as a marker for how you want the next 12 months at work to progress.

◗ Meditation booster

Recite the following sentence before you start your regular meditation: 'My wellbeing is my number one focus this month.'

◗ Ritual

Look at your diary and the week ahead and bless it.

◗ Things to do

- Renew your gym membership – or just start going again. Don't like the gym? Commit to walking regularly or doing yoga – anything that gets you moving.
- Think about your diet – it won't take care of itself.
- This House also rules service to others – so help someone out this month.
- Speak to your boss about any work concerns you have.
- Read a book about positive thinking.
- Eat healthy lunches or dinners for one month – no exceptions.
- Learn to meditate.

◗ Top 3 affirmations

Repeat one or all three daily during this New Moon, and in the coming four weeks.

1. 'I am more and more organized every day.'
2. 'I give wonderful service for wonderful pay.'
3. 'My wellbeing is my priority – I am getting back on track.'

◗ Essential oil

If you're having trouble expressing yourself, or you feel like your daily grind is all too much, try dabbing a bit of tea tree oil at the base of your throat or on your wrists, or putting it in your bath or burner.

◗ Numerological energy

The number 6 is the most harmonious of the numbers 1–9. It's the number of home, family and love, and it has a very loving and caring quality. It's also about giving up for others, nurturing, protecting and teaching, which is why it's also strongly associated with family, parenthood and motherhood.

◗ Mantra

Repeat the mantra *Hum* this month. Chant it out loud or silently every day: while you're in the shower, before or after meditating, or at any other time that feels right to you.

◗ Guiding Archangel

Metatron is one of only two Archangels who were once human prophets – along with the Pisces Archangel Sandalphon. Archangel Metatron was Enoch, the author of *The Book Of Enoch*, and is now known as the 'Scribe of God' and a teacher of esoteric knowledge. He's the first Archangel on the Tree of Life in the Kabbalah, which means that he helps people who are newly on the spiritual path.

For this reason, Metatron helps children to discover, increase and retain their spiritual gifts. Metatron also works hand in hand with your 6th House if and when you're healing or energy clearing. To connect with Archangel Metatron, simply light a candle, say the name Metatron, and ask for help:

'Dearest Archangel Metatron, please be with me this month as I work to clean up all aspects of my life. With your help and guidance, I can reach my full potential. Thank you.'

◗ Guiding Goddess

Ceres is the Roman Goddess of the Harvest. She's also known as the Goddess of Fertility and Motherly Relationships. To reap a harvest takes a lot of hard work and this is the part of your chart where you do the work. This part of the chart also rules our health, so talk to

Ceres if you're having health issues. Ask for guidance about your diet. Talk to her regarding fertility issues too.

◗ Universal Law

The law to contemplate this month is the Law of Compensation. Interestingly, this was the golden rule of Napoleon Hill (one of the earliest recognized personal success experts) – whatever we do, it'll come back to us. We reap what we sow. Or as Hill put it: 'When you start giving out, you'll soon begin taking in. The eternal Law of Compensation balances everything throughout the Universe.'

◗ Heavenly Ray

The 6th ray, which is indigo, is governed by Master Lanto and overseen by Saint Germain; it's a pure stream of devotion. This month, it's time to accept that the Creator's energy really does reside within your earthly body and reality.

This is a very inspirational energy that will allow you to connect more closely with the Divine, once you see that the Divine is in you. Small devotional rituals, such as incense lighting and practising yoga, will boost your connection.

New Moon (or solar eclipse) in your 7th House

(Also known as your Love Zone)

◗ It's all about…

Love and marriage, relationships, business partnerships, VIPs, friends and foes.

◗ What to expect

Issues related to love and relationships to come up, hopefully for sorting out.

◗ What to wish for

The best relationships you can have with all the people you know.

◗ What to visualize

See yourself face to face and palm to palm with someone you love or are in conflict with.

◗ Idea to keep in mind

'I am you and you are me. We're all one.' Even though the 7th House is all about our most important relationships, use this month to contemplate the idea that underneath all the egos and differences, we're all one; we're all connected to all life everywhere. It's a month to clean up your relationships.

◗ Messages

Your beloved (past, present or potential) is in focus at the time of this New Moon. Now is the time to think about all your relationships.

If you're attached, what can you do to make your love brand new? Do you still need to let go of the past? How confident do you feel about your love skills? Now is the time to go out on a blind date, if you're not in love and not having any luck with meeting someone new. If you can't let go of the past, call up your ex (if it feels right) for a chat and closure. See if you can work with your lover (past or present) now, as the 7th House is all about balance, cooperation and doing what's right.

◗ Meditation booster

Recite the following sentence before you start your regular meditation: 'I'll do what I know I need to do to feel more confident about love.'

◗ Ritual

Send a love note (or an email) to someone you love.

◗ Things to do

- Go through your old love letters – and get rid of at least some of them.
- If you're single and feeling brave, try online dating.
- Ask someone you know in a successful, committed relationship about about their ideas on how to make love work.
- Recommit to your partner.
- If you hurt a past lover, admit you were wrong and apologize to them.
- Make a list of the qualities you look for in a partner.
- If you're already attached, play matchmaker for a friend.

◗ Top 3 affirmations

Repeat one or all three daily during this New Moon, and in the coming four weeks.

1. 'I love you and I love me.'
2. 'I'm easy to get along with – all my relationships are harmonious.'
3. 'I'm free of the past. My relationships are now resolving themselves.'

◗ Essential oil

Jasmine is recommended for opening up the Heart chakra and it's therefore a wonderful oil with which to anoint yourself. You can dab a few drops around the area of your Heart chakra – in the middle of the chest, between the breasts – or pour it in your bath or put it in your burner, especially before meditating.

Numerological energy

This month's number, 7, is that of the seeker, the thinker and the person who needs to find things out for themselves. When you're in this cycle, seek the truth in all your relationships and situations, personal and professional. If you suspect things aren't as they seem, then this is the cycle to investigate.

Mantra

Use the mantra *Yum* this month. Chant it out loud or silently every day: while you're in the shower, before or after meditating, or at any other time that feels right to you.

Guiding Archangel

The Archangel Jophiel is the Archangel of Beauty. She's perfect as a guide as you contemplate your 7th House because she helps us to see others through the eyes of love. What could be better? Talk to Archangel Jophiel if you need help in a relationship. To connect with her, simply light a candle, say the name Jophiel, and ask for help:

> *'Dearest Archangel Jophiel, please be with me this month. With your help and guidance, my relationships, both personal and professional, can reach their full potential. Thank you.'*

Guiding Goddess

Lakshmi is the Hindu Goddess of love, wealth and beauty. The name 'Lakshmi' comes from the Sanskrit word '*Laksya*', meaning 'aim' or 'goal', and she's the go-to Goddess for any quests you have regarding wealth and prosperity, both material and spiritual. She's one of the most popular Goddesses. Print out a picture of her, and talk to her this month.

◗ Universal Law

The Universal Law to focus on this month is the best known of them all: the Law of Attraction. It reminds us, of course, that like attracts like. It shows us that we create the events and relationships that come into our lives. Every thought, feeling, word and action sets the Law of Attraction in motion, producing energies that attract like energies: positive or negative.

◗ Heavenly Ray

The 7th ray is governed by Lady Portia and overseen by Saint Germain. This is a very important ray as it's home to the famous violet flame of transmutation. This ray is hugely important to us because it raises consciousness and anchors a new age of awareness. Some have called it 'the awakening ray of light'. Visualize the colour violet as you fall asleep when the 7th House is being triggered.

New Moon (or solar eclipse) in your 8th House

(Also known as your Sex and Shared Finances Zone)

◗ It's all about…

Other people's money, and how it combines with yours.

◗ What to expect

A chance to inject newness into your finances or your sex life.

◗ What to wish for

More money! Better sex! To overcome a fear.

◗ What to visualize

What would you do if you had more cash? Visualize that. I'll let you take care of the sex-based visualization!

◗ Idea to keep in mind

Now is the time to attend to your cash set-up and see how good you feel about it. Are you confident that you're on track? Can you meet the bills you know you have ahead of you, and if not, is there something you can do now about that?

◗ Messages

This is a great time to seek financial advice, or to attend a business workshop to help you better understand the financial basics.

The part of your chart being triggered also deals with deep, dark and maybe even kinky sex. If you have intimacy issues that you know you need to work on, tackle them this month.

◗ Meditation booster

Recite the following sentence before you start your regular meditation: 'I tackle my cash problems head-on.'

◗ Ritual

Go out on the town wearing an outfit that you feel amazing in.

◗ Things to do

- Pay off a loan (or take one out).
- Open a savings account and make your first deposit.
- Cancel a credit card you know you can't afford.

- Ask for a pay rise (but only if you believe you might get it!).
- Refinance your mortgage, if it suits you.
- Talk dirty to your partner.
- Try a sexual position for the first time.

◗ Top 3 affirmations

Repeat one or all three daily during this New Moon, and in the coming four weeks:

1. 'I am taken care of materially.'
2. 'All my financial needs are being met.'
3. 'My sex life is so wonderfully healthy.'

◗ Essential oil

Myrrh helps us to become open to receiving gifts. As you use it, confirm that you're ready to receive.

◗ Numerological energy

The number 8 is the number of financial abundance and security. It's also the number of karma – we reap what we sow. Because the 8th House is in part about joint finances, it's about being honest in our dealings. This month reflect on what you are and aren't prepared to do for cash. This is also a very spiritual number.

◗ Mantra

Your mantra of the month is *Vam*. Chant it out loud or silently every day: while you're in the shower, before or after meditating, or at any other time that feels right to you.

Guiding Archangel

Jeremiel is one of the seven core Archangels. His main role is to help newly crossed-over souls review their lives. Jeremiel supports and guides people who have recently passed, as they review how their every action affected others, and what they learned during their lifetime. But you don't have to wait until you've crossed over to have a life review with Jeremiel, as this Archangel will help living people to take an inventory of their lives. All you have to do is ask for his help in this regard. To connect with Archangel Jeremiel, simply light a candle, say the name Jeremiel, and ask for help:

'Dearest Archangel Jeremiel, thank you for helping me to take a clear and honest inventory of my life. With your help, I see more clearly and feel empowered as I move forwards. Thank you.'

Guiding Goddess

Facing up to what scares us is a big part of this cycle and Kali – the blue Hindu Goddess with the scary face, aggressive stance and skulls – is the one to help us in this regard. Ask Kali to help you release negative people from your life, limiting thoughts, or any fears. Kali helps us to step away from our ego. She's also known as the Goddess who liberates our souls from the otherwise endless cycle of birth and death.

Universal Law

This month, the Law of Perpetual Transmutation of Energy reminds us that we all have the power to change the conditions of our lives. We just need to push through our fear and limiting thoughts: in particular negative thoughts directed at ourselves or others. Raise your vibration through yoga, chanting and meditating: higher vibrations transform lower ones. Pure sexual energy is a great transmuter.

◗ Heavenly Ray

The 8th ray, which is sea-foam green/aquamarine in colour, is governed by Lady Nada. It brings a deep spiritual cleansing that allows our soul to evolve. This works so well with the 8th House, which is a part of our chart where we may keep what we feel is 'unclean' about ourselves. Healing and cleansing is required to raise our vibrations. The 8th ray is made up of rays 4, 7 and 5 with a touch of white light.

New Moon (or solar eclipse) in your 9th House

(Also known as your Big Picture Zone)

◗ It's all about …

Adventure, travel and personal development.

◗ What to expect

New and potentially exciting developments related to travel, study, the internet, publishing and the Great Cosmic Quest.

◗ What to wish for

To see the bigger picture of your life and thus to invoke gratitude.

◗ What to visualize

Yourself wherever you'd most like to be on holiday!

◗ Idea to keep in mind

We're all Divine beings. The 9th House is strongly associated with the spiritual quest, as is Jupiter, the 9th House planet. The chakra that's traditionally associated with the 9th House is also about the Divine – it's the Crown chakra, which connects us to the heavens.

◗ Messages

The part of your chart being lit up by the New Moon is ruled by Jupiter, which is the planet of expansion. So whether you're expanding your mind by studying or travel, or by talking to well-travelled people, or through doing a personal development course, you have the chance now to broaden your horizons.

This cycle is also about your faith and beliefs. If you know you've been rigid – perhaps clinging on to what you were taught as a child rather than forming your own opinions – someone could come along now and either help or force you to rethink your philosophies. This is also a great time to break out of routines and to get a little more freedom.

◗ Meditation booster

Recite the following sentence before you start your regular meditation: 'Life's an adventure and I love it, so this month, I'll… (fill in the blank)'.

◗ Ritual

Decide on your next travel destination; put a picture of the place on your wall to remind yourself of your plans.

◗ Things to do

- Find a way to explore the world.
- Read those books you know you should.
- Take a personal development course.
- Manifest a new spiritual teacher.
- Think about what you have faith in – and what you don't.

- Make a cyber pal on the other side of the world.
- Have something you've written published.

Top 3 affirmations

Repeat one or all three daily during this New Moon, and in the coming four weeks:

1. 'I know that I am blessed.'
2. 'Life is an adventure!'
3. 'The world is my oyster!'

Essential oil

Sandalwood is a wonderful essential oil to use at this time. It's considered extremely sacred in Eastern religions and this is an especially sacred part of your chart. It's also great for spiritual awareness and for getting you in alignment with your soul purpose. These are some of the very big issues covered by the 9th House. Sandalwood is also an excellent meditation aid on any day of the week.

Numerological energy

The number 9 is about idealism – a trait that can go either way in terms of being a positive or a negative. Being idealistic can help us to make the world a better place. It implies a belief in a higher way of being. However, being too idealistic can cause issues. Look at where you're being an idealist during this cycle. The number 9 is the most tolerant and the most conscious number. Be *those things* this month.

◗ Mantra

Use the mantra *Ah* this month. Chant it out loud or silently every day: while you're in the shower, before or after meditating, or at any other time that feels right to you.

◗ Guiding Archangel

For Archangel Raguel, life is a party because he's the most sociable of all the Archangels. Raguel's name means 'Friend of God' and his focus is peace and harmony for everyone. Archangel Raguel also helps with resolving conflict. To connect with Archangel Raguel, simply light a candle, say the name Raguel, and ask for help:

> *'Dearest Archangel Raguel, please be with me this month as I live life to the fullest. With your help and guidance, I can reach my full potential and see the big picture. Thank you.'*

◗ Guiding Goddess

Fortuna is the Goddess of Fate and Chance, according to ye olde Latin proverb *Fortis fortuna adiuvat*, which means 'Fortuna, the Goddess of luck, favours those who take risks'. So if there's something you want during this cycle and you feel as though you'll have to take a bit of a risk to get it, Fortuna is your go-to Goddess. She's also the Goddess to talk to if you want to travel or study; she'll help you. Ask her to put good luck on your side.

◗ Universal Law

The Law of Relativity reminds us that all things are relative; that everything just 'is'. You'll always be not as good at some things as other people are, just as you'll have your own special talents. Don't measure yourself against other people. During this cycle, notice how you feel if you simply compare yourself with yourself.

Understand this law by understanding the notion that nothing is good or bad, or hot or cold or black or white, until you relate it to something else.

◗ Heavenly Ray

The 9th ray, which is blue-green, is the keeper of a treasure trove of knowledge that can aid in soul expansion. It's all about anchoring the joy that we feel when we love someone, be that romantic, familial or friendship love. It advances our move towards enlightenment and furthers the cleansing work of the 8th ray. It's composed of rays 1 and 2, and white light.

New Moon (or solar eclipse) in your 10th House

(Also known as your Career Zone)

◗ It's all about…

Your career and your reputation.

◗ What to expect

The chance to get ahead professionally.

◗ What to wish for

To help others through your work.

◗ What to visualize

Imagine yourself giving a talk, and being an expert at whatever you do.

◗ Idea to keep in mind

There's everything right with wanting to leave your mark on the world, or to be known for having done something. Whether you're ambitious to be a great parent or a great friend or you want to do something more 'visible', it's okay to aim high.

◗ Messages

This New Moon is an important one for career-minded folk, because it's all about your professional life. It's a great time to start a new business and the time when your past efforts at the office could be rewarded – you have an increased chance of promotion now, if you've put in the hard work.

Even if you don't get an actual promotion, you're far more likely to be recognized for your efforts during the coming month. This is also a good time to think about your future and what you want for yourself. Are you headed in the right direction to achieve your aims, ambitions and goals, and if not, what can you do about it?

◗ Meditation booster

Recite the following sentence before you start your regular meditation: 'Hard work breeds long-term success for me.'

◗ Ritual

Write out your ideal job description and read it through every day this month.

◗ Things to do

- Speak to your boss about how you're doing.
- Help a colleague out of a rut.
- Check that you've not become status mad.
- Start a new business as close to the New Moon as you can.
- Apply for new jobs with confidence.

- When you've earned it, take the credit.
- Plot your next best career move.

◗ Top 3 affirmations

Repeat one or all three daily during this New Moon, and in the coming four weeks:

1. 'I am going places!'
2. 'It's wonderful to be so successful!'
3. 'I love seeing my plans work out!'

◗ Essential oil

Laurel is a wonderful essential oil to use during this cycle (in your bath or burner). It will help you to focus as you work because it aids concentration. It also motivates and boosts confidence.

◗ Numerological energy

The digits in the number 10 add up to 1, which reminds you that you can be number one. The number 10 also reminds you that working alone and working for yourself can be a good thing. However, if you know you're too much of a lone wolf professionally, then use the power of the New Moon's influence to do something about that.

◗ Mantra

Use the mantra *Ram* this month. Chant it out loud or silently every day: while you're in the shower, before or after meditating, or at any other time that feels right to you.

◗ Guiding Archangel

Archangel Azrael gently heals grief-stricken hearts from any form of loss. If you've had career issues in the past (and frankly, who hasn't?), then ask Azrael to help you to heal your hurts. The more emotional baggage you can throw overboard this month as you move through your 10th House New Moon cycle, the better off you'll be professionally this time next year. To connect with Archangel Azrael, simply light a candle, say the name Azrael, and ask for help:

'Dearest Archangel Azrael, please be with me this month as I strive to achieve my worldly ambitions. With your help and guidance, I can reach my full potential when it comes to my professional life. Thank you.'

◗ Guiding Goddess

Juno is the Goddess of Time and Commitment. When you make a commitment, be it personal or professional, and you stick to it, you're fast-tracking yourself to success. Juno can help with this. This might not sound like the sexiest talent in the Universe, but in a world full of flakes, it makes Juno a Goddess worth knowing. It also translates to your personal life – for example, you know that relationships take work and you're willing to make the effort and do what you said you'd do. Work on your commitment this coming month.

◗ Universal Law

This month's law is the Law of Polarity. There are two poles – two opposites – of everything here on Earth or in the earthly realm. Polarity represents two extremes of one thing, or two opposite ends of a spectrum. So for example, temperature ranges from hot to cold. Measurements go from up to down, high to low, and things are on or off, or in or out. If you're not happy where you are, then move along the scale to where you want to be. Focus on what you do want, don't focus on what you don't want.

◗ Heavenly Ray

This month's ray is a combination of rays 1, 2 and 4, and is pearlescent (gold) in colour. It's governed by Lady and Master Andromeda and overseen by the Divine Director of the Rays. It helps our souls to integrate and unify with the Creator and allows humans to make the changes in themselves that they're seeking.

New Moon (or solar eclipse) in your 11th House

(Also known as your Friends Zone)

◗ It's all about…

Your friends and social networks (and your hopes and dreams).

◗ What to expect

The chance for a wish to come true, or for a friendship to blossom.

◗ What to wish for

Anything you want!

◗ What to visualize

Yourself, with your wish coming true, or surrounded by friends.

◗ Idea to keep in mind

There's no need to go through life alone. If you're spiritually evolved enough to be reading this, you're able to go out into the world and make friends. The 11th House brings to mind the expression 'no man [or woman] is an island'.

◗ Messages

This month, focus on your hopes and dreams. It's said that when the Sun moves through your 11th House – as it's doing now – your powers of wishing are supercharged. In other words, be extra careful what you wish for now, because you might get it.

Also focus on your friends and networks – the groups you belong to. How confident do you feel about your place within those groups? Are your needs being met, and if they're not, what can you do about it? New friends are extra likely to come into your life now.

◗ Meditation booster

Recite the following sentence before you start your regular meditation: 'The friendly people find the friendly people every time.'

◗ Ritual

Throw a party at your place. Yes, this is a valid ritual. Do it *consciously*.

◗ Things to do

- Sign up for an evening class in something you've always wanted to do.
- Ask your friends to introduce you to friends of theirs you've never met.
- Wish on a star every night for a month.
- Introduce a childhood pal to a friend from your life now.
- Say 'Hi' to someone you see often but never speak to.
- Thank your best friend for being there for you.

◗ Top 3 affirmations

Repeat one or all three daily during this New Moon, and in the coming four weeks:

1. 'I am connected to all life everywhere.'
2. 'I love my friends and my friends love me.'
3. 'My dreams are now manifesting under grace in perfect ways.'

◗ Essential oil

Chemical compounds found in frankincense essential oil can cross the blood–brain barrier and oxygenate the pineal gland. This little gland in our brain was called 'the seat of our soul' by great French philosopher René Descartes and is believed by some to be the often-referenced 'third eye'.

◗ Numerological energy

Your number for the month is the Master Number 11, which is one of the most powerful numbers of all. It represents knowing what's right, what to do, where to go with your life. This number walks the fine line between having and losing it all. This month, keep an eye out for 11s and go for gold in your life. The number 11 sees the world as full of opportunities and isn't afraid to boldly chase what it wants.

◗ Mantra

Om is this month's mantra. Chant it out loud or silently every day: while you're in the shower, before or after meditating, or at any other time that feels right to you.

◗ Guiding Archangel

In some ways, illuminating Archangel Uriel is like the wise old uncle who's always teaching those around him (think of Yoda from *Star Wars*, who wants to pass on all that he knows to the people around him). To connect with Archangel Uriel, simply light a candle, say the name Uriel, and ask for help:

'Dearest Archangel Uriel, please be with me this month as I explore my friendships and connections with people. With your help and guidance, I can reach my full potential when it comes to being a part of my community. Thank you.'

◗ Guiding Goddess

Isis is an eclectic but very famous Goddess. She mingled with the wealthy, the great and the good, and the innocent, but she was also a friend to slaves and sinners, artists and the downtrodden. Isis knew how to reach out and she's a wonderful Goddess to relate to at any time. Ask Isis for help if you need to widen your reach out in the world. Just light a candle and talk to her.

◗ Universal Law

The Law of Rhythm reminds us that the earthly plane moves in a certain rhythm. These rhythms establish the rhythms of life here on Earth: the seasons, the tides, the Moon phases, the female menstrual cycle, stages of human development. According to a book called *The Kybalion*, this accounts for 'the bewildering succession of moods, feelings and other annoying and perplexing changes that we notice in ourselves'.

The Hermetic Masters inspired by Hermes Trismegistus (aka the father of astrology) advised that by studying and understanding this principle, our 'bewildering' emotions and moods can be mastered.

◗ Heavenly Ray

The pink-orange 11th ray is a combination of rays 1, 2 and 5; it's governed by Lady Kuan Yin and overseen by the Divine Director of the Rays. It completes the process of merging the soul with God/dess, teaches about the power of love to manifest matter and helps us to connect to Divine love and wisdom. It balances male and female polarities.

New Moon (or solar eclipse) in your 12th House

(Also known as your Secrets Zone)

◗ It's all about...

Your secret and most private self.

◗ What to expect

A few weeks when you'll want to retreat from the world.

◗ What to wish for

Inner peace.

◗ What to visualize

Yourself in a cosmic pink bubble – at one with the Universe.

◗ Idea to keep in mind

It's okay to take time out to meditate and contemplate. It's been a year since the giver of life, the Sun, was in your sign. By now you may feel as though you're running low on power. Use this month to process what has gone on in the past 12 months and what you want for the year ahead, when the Sun crosses your ascendant (your rising sign) and moves back into your 1st House next month.

Messages

You know when you read astrology and it says something spooky like 'trust your dreams'? That's what I'm saying here. When the New Moon is in your 12th House, it's energizing the part of your chart that relates to dreams, and to all things secret and spooky. The part of your chart being triggered affects the side of yourself that you don't tell others about; it's about your secret self, your shadow side and your unconscious self.

Trusting your dreams is a great idea now because the Moon in this part of your chart can bring so much to the surface that's worth investigating. Because the part of your chart being triggered is also about all things spooky, it's also a great time to get in touch with your spiritual side by doing things like yoga and meditation. Sure, yoga exercises the body, but both yoga and meditation also calm the mind and help you get closer to your core self. This is the end of another cycle, so let go of what isn't working from your life to make room.

Meditation booster

Recite the following sentence before you start your regular meditation: 'My dreams are my guide.'

Ritual

Write a list of your fears and then burn it.

Things to do

- Make like a yogi and bend yourself into a pretzel.
- Take time out from the mad social whirl.
- Keep your phone near your bed and dictate your dreams into it when you awaken.

- Face one big fear. Deal with it by thinking about where it came from.
- Trust your intuition.
- Listen to calming meditation music every day for a month.
- Write poetry from the heart.
- Share one of your secrets.

Top 3 affirmations

Repeat one or all of these daily during this New Moon, and in the coming four weeks:

1. 'It's okay to say no.'
2. 'Inner peace is my focus.'
3. I now release my fears.'

Essential oil

This part of the chart is associated with fear and other negatives. Lavender is a powerful essential oil to work with to counter any fear, depression, anxiety or nervousness. It's great to work though such issues when the Moon is triggering your 12th House.

Numerological energy

This month's number is 12/3 – the epitome of wisdom. The Sun and Moon have now met up in all 12 of the Houses on your birth chart. You've evolved so much since the cycle began 12 months ago. The number 12/3 is fittingly associated with the Empress in Tarot, and also with the Hanged Man. This New Moon cycle isn't the time for you to be rushing around trying to start new projects. Rather, allow life to pass you by for once. Rest and recuperate. Next month is the time to launch new ventures.

◗ Mantra

Use the mantra *Ah* this month. Chant it out loud or silently every day: while you're in the shower, before or after meditating, or at any other time that feels right to you.

◗ Guiding Archangel

Sandalphon's energies are soft and gentle. His messages to you come as soft whispers that are easy to miss if you're not listening carefully. If you're talking to Sandalphon and asking for help, stay aware of meaningful songs you may hear. The lyrics could contain the angelic messages that Sandalphon wants you to hear. To connect with Archangel Sandalphon, simply light a candle, say the name Sandalphon, and ask for help:

> *'Dearest Archangel Sandalphon, please be with me this month as I reflect on the past 12 months. With your help and guidance, I can reach my full potential. Thank you.'*

◗ Guiding Goddess

Kuan Yin is one of the most famous of all the Goddesses and is renowned most of all for her compassion and mercy. In some cultures, she's the ideal of woman. She's said to have forgone the bliss of Nirvana to continue her role of helping humans. Kuan Yin carries Goddess and Divine Mother energy.

◗ Universal Law

According to the Law of Gender, every thing, person and situation has a male and female energy. This is how creation happens. The Universe was formed under the Law of Gender. To truly know yourself and to master the Universe you must live out both your masculine and feminine energies, whatever your gender identity. Then you can cocreate with God/dess.

Heavenly Ray

The 12th ray is governed by Pallas Athena and overseen by the Divine Director of the Rays and Lord Maitreya. This golden ray anchors Christ Consciousness, aka The Great Central Sun. It's a combination of all the rays plus white light, and has a wonderful golden luminosity.

Summary

You now have all you need in order to work with the New Moon. In this section you learned that:

- Manifesting in tune with the New Moon supercharges dreams and wishes.
- The meaning of the New Moon through all 12 signs.
- What the New Moon through all 12 Houses means for you personally.

FAQs: the New Moon

Here's my response to some of the more general questions I'm asked about the subjects covered in this section:

Must I wish in accordance with each sign/House?

No! Every month you can wish for whatever you want. However, ideally, you'd make a couple of wishes in accordance with the sign and House, as those wishes will be supercharged. Also, doing this means that after one year, you'll have wished about, set intentions and/or worked on every part of your life, since every part of your life is covered in your chart.

◗ Do I have a personal New Moon?

Your personal New Moon takes place once a month, when the transiting Moon moves over your Sun. This happens during the two and a bit days when the Moon is in your star sign. It can be a more emotional time than usual, especially if you're a Water sign (Cancer, Scorpio or Pisces). Overall though, it's a good personal marker. Check in with yourself and your New Moon wishes, and see if you're on track to make your dreams come true.

To know when your personal New Moon is happening, you need to keep an eye on the Daily Moon (*see Part IV*). You know that when it moves into the sign you were born under – for example, Leo if you're a Leo, Capricorn if you're a Capricorn and so on – then within the next two and a bit days, you'll experience your personal New Moon.

◗ Is there ever more than one New Moon in a House?

You'll usually have one New Moon in each of the 12 Houses – so once a year in your 1st House, once a year in your 2nd House and so on. When you get a rare two New Moons in a House within the space of two months, there's a reason for that. You're either being directed to focus more on that part of your life and making changes, or you might be getting something like a second chance on making good on the House/part of your life that's in focus and which you're hopefully working on.

◗ Is there a special New Moon for wishing?

Yes! The annual New Moon in your 11th House – which is also known as the House of Hope and Wishes – is superpowered when it comes to making New Moon wishes. And if a New Moon eclipse happens to take place in your 11th House, all that goes quadruple.

As far as timing is concerned, I could just say: 'Make your New Moon wishes every month and you'll eventually be making them when the New Moon is in your 11th House.' However, I believe it's good to be prepared, so here is a quick guide to which New Moon is your superpowered-wishing New Moon and therefore extra important to harness. *Be sure to make your wishes at each one.* You can use your star sign if you don't know your rising sign. (Tip: If you don't have the list below handy when working this out, remember it's the New Moon in the sign that's two before your star sign or rising sign.)

Find your superpowered-wishing New Moon			
♈	Aries or Aries rising	♒	Aquarius New Moon
♉	Taurus or Taurus rising	♓	Pisces New Moon
♊	Gemini or Gemini rising	♈	Aries New Moon
♋	Cancer or Cancer rising	♉	Taurus New Moon
♌	Leo or Leo rising	♊	Gemini New Moon
♍	Virgo or Virgo rising	♋	Cancer New Moon
♎	Libra or Libra rising	♌	Leo New Moon
♏	Scorpio or Scorpio rising	♍	Virgo New Moon
♐	Sagittarius or Sagittarius rising	♎	Libra New Moon
♑	Capricorn or Capricorn rising	♏	Scorpio New Moon
♒	Aquarius or Aquarius rising	♐	Sagittarius New Moon
♓	Pisces or Pisces rising	♑	Capricorn New Moon

◗ What if a New/Full Moon falls on my birthday?

A New Moon on your birthday is a big sign from the Universe that exciting developments and changes lie ahead. It's as though you're getting a massive injection of new energy from the Universe. Bear in mind that if the New Moon takes place on or just before your birthday, you're actually having the New Moon on your Sun – i.e. in the same spot where the Sun was on the day you were born.

It's big and exciting, and if there's a New Moon eclipse on your birthday, all that goes triple and on steroids!

What if a New or Full Moon falls on my birthday?

a New Moon on your birthday [illegible] after sign from the planets that exciting developments and changes lie ahead [illegible] [illegible] getting a massive injection of new energy from the Universe. [illegible] [illegible] the New Moon takes place on or just before your birthday, you [illegible] having the New Moon in your sun sign [illegible] the same [illegible] as the Sun was in when you were born.

[illegible]

PART III

Work with The Magic of The Full Moon

The Full Moon is the high point of the lunar cycle. It's a very powerful time for inner work – for looking within, healing, shifting blocks and shedding the past: things we all need to do on a regular basis.

CHAPTER 6

Full Moon Forgiveness and Gratitude

The Full Moon is seen as the 'climax' of the monthly lunar cycle. Of course, the lunar cycle never actually 'ends' – at least it hasn't to date. Rather, the Moon is forever waxing and waning. The energies build and build and build from the New Moon to the Full Moon and then... bang! There's some Full Moon madness when emotional explosions are possible, followed by a sort of cosmic lunar sigh. At the time of the Full Moon we're being asked (forced) to deal with our 'stuff', which, as I mentioned earlier, is why some people can get a bit emotional.

The Full Moon then is all about peaking and releasing the old: letting go of lower energies that come from upsets or any negative events, as well as negative patterns you may have fallen into. It's about releasing toxic thoughts, habits, ways of being and, indeed, toxic people. It's culmination time. It's letting-go and clean-slate time. It's when we should release the things we don't want: guilt, fear, disappointment, jealousy – anything that's counterproductive.

The Full Moon is also a powerful time for inner work – for looking within, healing, shifting blocks and shedding the past. When the Moon is full, it's at its brightest and it can shine a light on our darkness – on the deepest parts of ourselves that we usually can't see.

The Full Moon also creates something of a tug-of-war in us. We have the Sun in one half of our horoscope chart and the Moon on the exact other side. We see where things are out of balance and bring them back into harmony. Working too hard? The Full Moon reminds us to pay some attention in our working life. Spending too much? Events at the time of the Full Moon can remind us to rein things in. Giving too much? The Full Moon is the time to remember to take as well. And so on.

Why forgiveness is crucial for manifesting

It's important to note that in order to realize our dreams via New Moon manifesting, we need to have released any grudges or upsets that we have against anyone. That's just how it works. The Full Moon is also the ideal time to practise forgiveness and gratitude. We can use the Full Moon to process the following:

- Negative emotions
- Fears
- Upsets
- Arguments
- Disappointments
- Dramas
- Wrongdoings

And in order to process (and release the karma that goes with whatever has happened), we have to forgive. That might mean forgiving ourselves, or forgiving someone else. Sounds challenging? Not necessarily.

Imagine that before you came down here to Earth, before you incarnated, you made several soul agreements. You knew that you wanted your soul to evolve during your lifetime, so you made agreements with other souls to 'do things to each other' that would push all your buttons, maybe even push you to the edge, but mainly would teach you.

So, if and when someone really upsets you and pushes all your buttons and starts to test you, imagine they're someone with whom you have a soul contract. Look for the lessons that the upset is teaching you. Think of it as a set-up designed to help you evolve, rather than an up-set. Get it? Learn the lesson and you'll be able to move on.

If we accept that we're on this planet to evolve, so that we no longer have to keep reincarnating, we'll perhaps try harder to handle the issues we come up against. That friend who really annoys you turns out to be your teacher. That stranger who was rude to you? Also your teacher. That teacher back at school who was mean to you and made you feel bad? Your teacher. Your lover, your ex, 'The One That Got Away'? Your teachers. Your kids? Your teachers.

So, once a month, at the time of the Full Moon, we take a moment to 'get square' with our teachers. We forgive them for what they've done because they have a soul contract with us, whether they know it or not. Most people are doing their best, even if it sometimes doesn't appear that way to us, so we might as well give them credit for that.

And resentment only leads to bitterness, which is toxic. As the Buddha allegedly said (although some people attribute the words to the Buddhist teacher Pema Chödrön), 'Holding on to anger is like drinking poison and expecting the other person to die.'

Full Moon Timings

If you check the times and dates of future Full Moons (timeanddate.com/moon/phases is a great resource), you'll notice that the Full Moon doesn't always take place at night. Sometimes, for example, it takes place at 10 a.m. or 3 p.m. or literally any time of the day. The best time to do your Full Moon forgiveness work is the night *before* the Full Moon rather than the night *after* it.

~

Remember, at Full Moon time, all our feelings swell, just like the Moon. That's why Full Moon can be such an emotional time. The problem is we're mostly not taught about this, so we either act out or try to push these emotions back down, hoping they'll go away (which of course they don't!). In Moonology, at the Full Moon, we take a moment to feel all these feelings, so that we can better process them. Since our emotions are coming up to the surface anyway, we might as well access them and release them, right?

There's another benefit to doing this: the Law of Attraction states that like attracts like, so if we're filled with upsets, then what do we attract? More upsets. Forgiving and releasing allows us to empty out upsets and replace them with gratitude. In doing so, we start to attract more to be grateful for.

Forgiveness isn't always easy, but it's been shown to have multiple benefits: healthier relationships; improved mental health; less anxiety, stress and hostility; fewer symptoms of depression; lower blood pressure; a stronger immune system; improved heart health and improved self-esteem.[‡]

‡ Mayo Clinic (2022), 'Forgiveness: Letting go of grudges and bitterness': www.mayoclinic.org/healthy-lifestyle/adult-health/in-depth/forgiveness/art-20047692 [Accessed 10 November 2025]

How to forgive someone

It could be argued that being angry is better than feeling helpless and hopeless. However, anger should be seen merely as a stepping stone on the way back to wellness – which is when you no longer harbour any upset against someone.

Sometimes you can forgive and forget. Sometimes you can only forgive but you can't forget. And sometimes you can forgive but it's not even wise to forget. We're all human and we all make mistakes; we're all fighting our own personal battles.

And just to repeat: Forgiving someone for what they did does *not* make what they did right. It means you've dealt with it and can now move on. When we're upset with someone – when we're furious, or bitter or twisted – we start to shut down our functions. The signals we're sending out are more in tune with our anger than they are with anything else. And these signals have a big impact on how our life unfolds. Remember, according to the Law of Attraction, like attracts like.

So when we're angry, we're giving out bad vibes. When we forgive, we give out much cleaner, purer and happier vibes, and when we do that, it's much easier to manifest our dreams.

Here's a simple Full Moon forgiveness ceremony that, very gently, will help you to open up a release valve. Some upsets will need to be processed just once, but others will take more than one Full Moon.

☾ Full Moon Forgiveness Ceremony

1. Take some deep, cleansing breaths. Release any stress, worries or cares as you exhale.
2. Think back to or reread your New Moon wishes. What has manifested for you this month and what hasn't? Be grateful for wishes that came true and congratulate yourself on your manifesting. Where something hasn't materialized, release

it to the Divine now. You can come back to it next New Moon – or perhaps the Universe has a better plan for you. And breathe. Sit with this and feel your trust that all will be well, everything is as it's meant to be and what's meant for you won't pass you by...

3. Now comes the life-changing part: Take a moment to *feel* your feelings. Where do you have emotional discomfort or pain? The Full Moon is a powerful time for emotional release. Who or what do you need to forgive, or make peace with or release? (You can go right back to your childhood, to anyone you haven't yet forgiven).

   Often, we need to forgive ourselves for something. Maybe you just need to process an upset. Bring it to your consciousness, come to terms with it as much as you can, forgive it as much as you can and let it all go under the Full Moon, which aids and abets this process. Writing it down will help hugely. You can literally 'express' it... and let it go.

   Take as much time as you need to release. Breathe out. Remember that forgiveness doesn't mean that what happened was okay, just that you're ready to move on. And remember that doing this will make you a more powerful manifester!

4. If there's someone in particular (or several people) you need to forgive, close your eyes and visualize that person/those people. See them (or yourself) inside a pink bubble in your mind's eye (pink is one of the colours of love). See them smiling at you. Create a good feeling between the two of you. Say silently or out loud: 'I forgive you,' and then let them float off in their bubble. If you're forgiving yourself, visualize yourself in this pink bubble and say silently or out loud: 'I forgive me.' You may even want to hug yourself as you forgive yourself.

5. Now recite the following Full Moon Forgiveness and Karma Release Formula:

> *'Under the glorious Full Moon, I forgive everything, everyone, every experience, every memory of the past or present that needs forgiveness. I forgive positively everyone. I also forgive myself of past mistakes. The Universe is love, and I am forgiven and governed by love alone. Love is now adjusting my life. Realizing this, I abide in peace.'*

You may wish to add:

> *'I bring love and healing to all my thoughts, beliefs and relationships. I learn my lessons and move on. I call on my soul fragments to be cleansed by the Full Moon and to rejoin me. I send love to myself and everyone I know, and everyone who knows me, in all directions of time. Under this glorious Full Moon, I am healed. My life is healed. And so it is. So be it.'*

6. If you wrote a forgiveness list, it's crucial to burn it (safely!). Doing this releases the energies into the ether for transmutation into love.

~

The importance of gratitude

In performing the above ceremony, and writing your forgiveness list, you're releasing resentment. Gratitude is the ideal quality to replace resentment. It raises your vibration, so you'll be happier; and the higher and clearer your vibration, the better you'll be able to manifest in two weeks' time at the New Moon .

Entering a State of Gratitude Ceremony

When you're in a state of gratitude, you can manifest extra well. This is because being in this state closes down your ego, which might otherwise bring in doubts while you're manifesting.

1. Take a moment to think of at least three people, places, situations or things for which you're grateful. Really feel gratitude in your body!
2. Write a list of who/what you're grateful for.
3. Burn your gratitude list after writing it. You just want to let things go at this time of the month.
4. Finally, if it feels right for you, say this incantation: 'I know that I am blessed and I live my life within that knowing.'

~

CHAPTER 7

Plan Your Life with the Full Moon

Practising Full Moon forgiveness and gratitude, and their associated ceremonies, is always a good idea. But for hardcore Moon lovers, there's more to do at the time of the Full Moon. Like the New Moon, the Full Moon takes place in a different sign of the zodiac each month. And as you now know, each sign offers a different vibration and range of themes for us to work with. You can use your heightened emotions at the time of the Full Moon to ask yourself some hard questions!

A guide to the Full Moon in each sign

The information in this chapter applies to *all of us,* regardless of our personal astrology. Each Full Moon is a lunation in a particular sign, and it therefore has a flavour of its own, no matter which star sign or rising sign we are.

To find out when the next Full Moon will occur, first visit timeanddate.com/moon/phases, then go to my home page – yasminboland.com – to find out which sign the Moon will be in. Then read on to discover all you need to know to work consciously with the Full Moon energies, including:

- The top 5 questions to ask yourself at the Full Moon.
- The message of each Full Moon according to the sign it falls in.
- The parts of your life where you need to find a balance – note that the Sun and the Moon are on opposite sides of the skies at the time of the Full Moon and this creates a tension that needs to be addressed.
- It also asks you to practise forgiveness by performing the 'Full Moon forgiveness ceremony' on the night of the Full Moon, and to practise gratitude by doing the 'Entering a state of gratitude ceremony' (*see pages 143 and 146*).

As with the New Moon through the signs, the following information about the Full Moon through the signs can also apply to lunar eclipses, aka Full Moon eclipses, through the signs. Once again, keep in mind the main themes of each Full Moon, and double their power if and when the Full Moon happens to be an eclipse. Also note that the Full Moon forgiveness and gratitude ceremonies mentioned in Chapter 6 (*see pages 143 and 146*) are extra powerful at the time of an eclipse. Think of it like this: eclipses supercharge lunations; Full Moons are intense; Full Moon eclipses are really intense!

Full Moon (or lunar eclipse) in Aries ♈

This Full Moon is especially good for Aries, Geminis, Leos, Librans, Sagittarians and Aquarians, but it's more challenging for everyone else.

◗ The energy is…

Fiery and rash.

◗ Top 5 questions

1. Have I been hot-headed, selfish or argumentative this month?
2. Have I been going too fast or been impulsive this month?
3. Have I been brash, blunt or too competitive?
4. Have I ignored other people's finer sensibilities?
5. Have I had enough fun?

◗ Message

Life isn't a race or a competition.

◗ Find a balance between…

Your needs and those of your significant other or best friend(s).

◗ Forgive

Perform the 'Full Moon forgiveness ceremony' on page 143. Write your forgiveness list and then burn it.

◗ Be grateful

Perform the 'Entering a state of gratitude ceremony' on page 146. Write your gratitude list and then burn it.

Full Moon (or lunar eclipse) in Taurus ♉

This Full Moon is especially good for Taureans, Cancerians, Virgos, Scorpios, Capricorns and Pisceans, but it's more challenging for everyone else.

◗ The energy is…

Earthy and steady.

◗ Top 5 questions

1. Have I been lazy or overly self-indulgent this month?
2. Have I been too obsessed with money or status symbols?
3. Have I been stubborn, jealous or possessive?
4. Have I been doing too much comfort-eating?
5. Have I done enough exercise?

◗ Message

Re-energize your life.

◗ Find a balance between…

All your feelings and what you can practically do about life.

◗ Forgive

Perform the 'Full Moon forgiveness ceremony' on page 143. Write your forgiveness list and then burn it.

◗ Be grateful

Perform the 'Entering a state of gratitude ceremony' on page 146. Write your gratitude list and then burn it.

Full Moon (or lunar eclipse) in Gemini ♊

This Full Moon is especially good for Aries, Geminis, Leos, Librans, Sagittarians and Aquarians, but it's more challenging for everyone else.

◗ The energy is…

Changeable and fickle.

◗ Top 5 questions

1. Have I been gossipy, superficial or flighty this month?
2. Have I been glossing over other people's feelings?
3. Have I been too quick to change my mind, or too restless?
4. Have I been too much of a silver-tongued hustler?
5. Have I done enough reading to keep expanding my mind?

◗ Message

Slow down and be real with people.

◗ Find a balance between…

Wanting to know everything and taking the time to really learn.

◗ Forgive

Perform the 'Full Moon forgiveness ceremony' on page 143. Write your forgiveness list and then burn it.

◗ Be grateful

Perform the 'Entering a state of gratitude ceremony' on page 146. Write your gratitude list and then burn it.

Full Moon (or lunar eclipse) in Cancer ♋

This Full Moon is especially good for Taureans, Cancerians, Virgos, Scorpios, Capricorns and Pisceans, but it's more challenging for everyone else.

◗ The energy is…

Dependent and possibly needy.

◗ Top 5 questions

1. Have I been insecure, clingy and no fun this month?
2. Have I been coming at what I want sideways, instead of tackling it head-on?
3. Have I been sulky, moody, brooding or manipulative? Hmmm?
4. Have I been secretive and possibly even a tad paranoid?
5. Have I had enough family time, or time with people who feel like family?

◗ Message

Feel sure of yourself.

◗ Find a balance between…

Your need to achieve, and your need for quality time at home.

◗ Forgive

Perform the 'Full Moon forgiveness ceremony' on page 143. Write your forgiveness list and then burn it.

◗ Be grateful

Perform the 'Entering a state of gratitude ceremony' on page 146. Write your gratitude list and then burn it.

Full Moon (or lunar eclipse) in Leo ♌

This Full Moon is especially good for Aries, Geminis, Leos, Librans, Sagittarians and Aquarians, but it's more challenging for everyone else.

◗ The energy is…

Bright and proud – maybe too proud!

◗ Top 5 questions

1. Have I been too self-centred, egotistical or proud?
2. Have I been treating the people around me like minions?
3. Have I been arrogant, vain, pushy or pompous?
4. Have I been expressing myself creatively enough?
5. Have I shown myself enough self-love?

◗ Message

The Leo Full Moon is a good time to get back in touch with our humility.

◗ Find a balance between…

What your friends need and what you need.

◗ Forgive

Perform the 'Full Moon forgiveness ceremony' on page 143. Write your forgiveness list and then burn it.

◗ Be grateful

Perform the 'Entering a state of gratitude ceremony' on page 146. Write your gratitude list and then burn it.

Full Moon (or lunar eclipse) in Virgo ♍

This Full Moon is especially good for Taureans, Cancerians, Virgos, Scorpios, Capricorns and Pisceans, but it's more challenging for everyone else.

◗ The energy is…

Finicky and anxious.

◗ Top 5 questions

1. Have I been too picky, pedantic or critical of myself or anyone else?
2. Have I been humble to the point of underrating myself?
3. Have I been of service to others enough this month?
4. Have I been worrying and complaining too much, and thus attracting negativity?
5. Have I paid enough attention to the details this month?

◗ Message

Remember the importance of being helpful to others.

◗ Find a balance between…

Being down to earth and allowing yourself to dream!

◗ Forgive

Perform the 'Full Moon forgiveness ceremony' on page 143. Write your forgiveness list and then burn it.

◗ Be grateful

Perform the 'Entering a state of gratitude ceremony' on page 146. Write your gratitude list and then burn it.

Full Moon (or lunar eclipse) in Libra ♎

This Full Moon is especially good for Aries, Geminis, Leos, Librans, Sagittarians and Aquarians, but it's more challenging for others.

◗ The energy is…

Focused on relationships and partnerships.

◗ Top 5 questions

1. Have I been too concerned with appearance in general?
2. Have I been thinking too much about others and neglecting my own needs?
3. Have I been too easily influenced, gullible or unable to decide for myself?
4. Have I been living my life through someone else?
5. Have I spent enough time beautifying my life?

◗ Message

Remind yourself to see the beauty in life.

◗ Find a balance between…

What you need and what you need to do for others.

◗ Forgive

Perform the 'Full Moon forgiveness ceremony' on page 143. Write your forgiveness list and then burn it.

◗ Be grateful

Perform the 'Entering a state of gratitude ceremony' on page 146. Write your gratitude list and then burn it.

Full Moon (or lunar eclipse) in Scorpio ♏

This Full Moon is especially good for Taureans, Cancerians, Virgos, Scorpios, Capricorns and Pisceans, but it's more challenging for everyone else.

◗ The energy is…

Potentially rather intense!

◗ Top 5 questions

1. Have I been jealous, vengeful, suspicious or otherwise behaved toxically?
2. Have I been living out of fear rather than joy?
3. Have I been focusing on the negative rather than the positive?
4. Have I been cruel or cunning?
5. Am I having the sex I need to feel good about myself? (Of course, some people need no sex at all!)

◗ Message

This is a good time to 'bring sexy back'.

◗ Find a balance between…

Over-intensity and lazy contentment.

◗ Forgive

Perform the 'Full Moon forgiveness ceremony' on page 143. Write your forgiveness list and then burn it.

◗ Be grateful

Perform the 'Entering a state of gratitude ceremony' on page 146. Write your gratitude list and then burn it.

Full Moon (or lunar eclipse) in Sagittarius ♐

This Full Moon is especially good for Aries, Geminis, Leos, Librans, Sagittarians and Aquarians, but it's more challenging for everyone else.

◗ The energy is…

Fun, and it may prompt many sighs of relief.

◗ Top 5 questions

1. Have I been too flippant, or carefree to the point of being careless, irresponsible, even?
2. Have I been letting myself down by allowing myself to get distracted and bored?
3. Have I been overconfident to the point of arrogance?
4. Have I been a commitment-phobe, to my own detriment?
5. Have I been seeing the bigger picture?

◗ Message

Life is an adventure. Don't stagnate!

◗ Find a balance between…

Speaking your mind and saying far too much.

◗ Forgive

Perform the 'Full Moon forgiveness ceremony' on page 143. Write your forgiveness list and then burn it.

◗ Be grateful

Perform the 'Entering a state of gratitude ceremony' on page 146. Write your gratitude list and then burn it.

Full Moon (or lunar eclipse) in Capricorn ♑

This Full Moon is especially good for Taureans, Cancerians, Virgos, Scorpios, Capricorns and Pisceans, but it's more challenging for everyone else.

◗ The energy is...

Repressed and resigned.

◗ Top 5 questions

1. Have I been ambitious to the point of ruthlessness?
2. Have I been obsessed with work to the detriment of my personal life?
3. Have I been hard-headed, hard-nosed or just too hard on others?
4. Have I allowed my head to overrule my heart?
5. Have I been planning my life enough? Or too much?

◗ Message

Release trying to control everything and everyone.

◗ Find a balance between...

The demands of work and home.

◗ Forgive

Perform the 'Full Moon forgiveness ceremony' on page 143. Write your forgiveness list and then burn it.

◗ Be grateful

Perform the 'Entering a state of gratitude ceremony' on page 146. Write your gratitude list and then burn it.

Full Moon (or lunar eclipse) in Aquarius ♒

This Full Moon is especially good for Aries, Geminis, Leos, Librans, Sagittarians and Aquarians, but it's more challenging for everyone else.

◗ The energy is…

Ushering in change and progress.

◗ Top 5 questions

1. Have I been pragmatic to the point of losing the romance of life?
2. Have I been living in my head rather than in my heart?
3. Have I been trying to do things my way, just for the sake of it?
4. Have I been trying too hard to befriend people, and for the wrong reasons?
5. Have I allowed myself to move forwards this month?

◗ Message

It's time to detach and let go. Really.

◗ Find a balance between…

Trying to be all things to all people vs having real relationships.

◗ Forgive

Perform the 'Full Moon forgiveness ceremony' on page 143. Write your forgiveness list and then burn it.

◗ Be grateful

Perform the 'Entering a state of gratitude ceremony' on page 146. Write your gratitude list and then burn it.

Full Moon (or lunar eclipse) in Pisces ♓

This Full Moon is especially good for Taureans, Cancerians, Virgos, Scorpios, Capricorns and Pisceans, but it's more challenging for everyone else.

◗ The energy is…

Nostalgic, and a little bit yearning.

◗ Top 5 questions

1. Have I been dreamy to the point of not getting enough done and making silly errors?
2. Have I been overly sensitive and too easily hurt?
3. Have I been acting like a martyr? Or too easily led?
4. Have I been meditating every day, and if not, why not?
5. Have I been in touch my intuitive side? Following my dreams and hunches?

◗ Message

This is a super mystical Moon – connect with your inner psychic.

◗ Find a balance between…

Your need for inner peace versus all your duties.

◗ Forgive

Perform the 'Full Moon forgiveness ceremony' on page 143. Write your forgiveness list and then burn it.

◗ Be grateful

Perform the 'Entering a state of gratitude ceremony' on page 146. Write your gratitude list and then burn it.

CHAPTER 8

Predict Your Future with the Full Moon

Once you know your rising sign (see moonologybook.com/freechart), have found out which *sign* the Full Moon is in at my site – yasminboland.com – and discovered which *House* that is for you (*see pages 84–85*), you'll be ready to look at what the Full Moon means for you personally, as it moves through the Houses.

A guide to the Full Moon in each House

What follows is a guide to how the Full Moon in each House affects you personally. The guide includes the following information:

- The messages of each Full Moon according to the House it falls in.
- An emotion alert! Full Moons can be emotional times so there's one of these for each House.
- As with the Full Moon in each sign, it's important to work with the two opposing energies that the Full Moon in each House brings up. These need balancing.

- The Full Moon is the time to release anything that no longer serves you. Knowing which House the Full Moon is in can act as a guide to what needs releasing.
- The opposition of the Sun and Moon at the time of the Full Moon can create a tug-of-war. Knowing which Houses the Full Moon is straddling can help you to foresee this.
- The mantra to say at the Full Moon.
- The affirmation to say at the Full Moon.

Full Moon (or lunar eclipse) in your 1st House

(Also known as your Image Zone)

◗ In the coming two weeks…

Expect to turn the corner in one way or another in your personal or professional life.

◗ Emotion alert!

The Full Moon can bring up intense feelings about your appearance, or stresses and strains in a relationship. It can be a big turning point.

◗ Messages

It's all very well and lovely to be focused on someone else – it certainly sounds like a valiant thing – but once a year, the Full Moon lights up your 1st House to remind you that you also need to focus on yourself.

Many of us are givers rather than takers, and while that sounds great, it actually messes with the flow in our lives. The Full Moon in your 1st House is the time to remember how to say 'yes' when people offer to help you, and to ask for help if you need it and you're not getting it. You could feel extra emotional during this cycle, but a lot of the 'stuff' that's coming up for you *needs* to be dealt with, so don't run away from it.

◗ Release any issues you have about…

Your appearance. That might sound superficial but it's amazing how feeling that we're too fat or too thin or too anything else can negatively impact our life and stop us from getting out there and reaching our full potential. Work on yourself and find at least one or two things about yourself that you know are totally gorgeous, no matter what other feelings you might have about your looks.

Focus on what you love. Play it up and revel in it. This is an important and somehow extra-personal Full Moon. Use it to work out what you want to take with you into your next 12-month life cycle, and what and who you want to leave behind. This can be a very emotional time.

◗ A tug-of-war may arise between…

Your needs and those of the people who are most important to you.

◗ Find a balance between…

Your lover or partner or ex, or anyone else in your life who counts as a VIP, and you. This can be a time when you realize you've been too focused on someone else and it's time to focus on yourself for a while. Or totally contrariwise, it can be a time when you realize you've been acting a little selfishly and need to give someone else your time and attention. It's all about me and you – much as it is in the 7th House Full Moon in six months' time. This is your chance to make a twice-yearly adjustment.

◗ Forgive…

Yourself.

◗ Be grateful

Write your gratitude list, and then burn it.

◗ Mantra

Use the mantra *Ram* this month. Chant it out loud or silently every day: while you're in the shower, before or after meditating, or at any other time that feels right to you.

◗ Affirmation

Say the following on the night of the Full Moon:

'I am turning the corner!'

Full Moon (or lunar eclipse) in your 2nd House

(Also known as your Cash, Property and Values Zone)

◗ In the coming two weeks...

Breathe through any financial dramas and focus on finding a solution.

◗ Emotion alert!

The Full Moon can bring up intense feelings about your financial security and stability, and about your self-worth.

◗ Messages

This Full Moon reminds you that a balance is needed between what you do for yourself financially and what you do for others. There's your income to be considered, and your debts. There's your self-worth and what you think you're worth as a person, and there's what others are willing to pay you – which is usually based on what you ask for, at least within reason.

If you're about to make a major purchase, you're doing it at the right time. If you've been letting someone control you because they have financial power over you, around about the time of your 2nd House Full Moon is your chance to break free. This Full Moon is also reminding you that you need to take care of your intimate life. Don't neglect it because of worldly concerns.

◗ Release any issues you have about…

Money. The 2nd House is all about cash, property and possessions. So at this time, there could be some kind of climax or conclusion connected to money. If you've been fearful regarding this lately, work with this Full Moon and the associated affirmation (*see page 166*) to release that tension. You can move into a better financial cycle now. One thing to be strongly aware of is that your self-esteem will affect how much money you attract.

◗ A tug-of-war may arise between…

Your own money and what other people pay you or owe you.

◗ Find a balance between…

Any issues you have regarding give and take. If you want to earn your own cash rather than be employed by someone else, this is a very good time to plan your exit strategy or cut the ties. If you've been too focused or dependent on someone else, now is the time to bring your attention back to your own situation. It's a good time to get your head around the idea that the Universe is abundant and that there's more than enough for everyone. You deserve to be abundant.

◗ Forgive…

Yourself and anyone else you need to, for times when money has been an issue.

◗ Be grateful

Make your gratitude list.

◗ Mantra

Use the mantra *Lam* this Full Moon. Chant it out loud or silently every day: while you're in the shower, before or after meditating, or at any other time that feels right to you.

◗ Affirmation

Say the following on the night of the Full Moon:

'All of my needs are met. I am worth it!'

Full Moon (or lunar eclipse) in your 3rd House

(Also known as your Communications Zone)

◗ In the coming two weeks...

You could say more than you mean to.

◗ Emotion alert!

The Full Moon can bring up intense feelings about siblings and neighbours. And about whether or not you should be honest about how you feel.

◗ Messages

It's all very well dreaming of the Great Escape – where you and possibly a loved one or two decide to take off to see the world (or at least the nearby countryside) – but what about the details? This Full Moon reminds you that there's a lot of work to be done close to home: things that need taking care of, and items on your to-do list to be ticked off.

It's also a celestial reminder that you seriously need to express yourself. If you haven't been honest about how you feel, now is the time to start saying your piece: whether you're talking face to face, messaging online or whatever. Dramas with siblings are highlighted now and can be sorted out.

◗ Release any issues you have about…

Communication, your sibling(s) and/or neighbours. Be extra careful not to allow disagreements to escalate out of control. For some, the Full Moon here will reveal the information that's needed to solve a long-standing problem or query.

Be careful what you write down on paper, in an email, in a text, on social media or anywhere else at this time. Emotions are running high, so don't hit 'send' and then regret it. Problems with siblings and neighbours can come to a head now too. Issues can be resolved with forgiveness. Remember, it's often less what you say than how you say it.

◗ A tug-of-war may arise between…

Where you are and where you think you'd like to be.

◗ Find a balance between…

Your own backyard and the big wide world out there. This is also a Full Moon that can trigger some kind of development or resolution regarding a legal issue. Distant friends and relatives can loom larger, as can trips away and job opportunities abroad. Where do you want to be? Here or there?

◗ Forgive…

Yourself for any negative words you've spoken; forgive your neighbours and siblings for any upsets.

◗ **Be grateful**

Make your gratitude list.

◗ **Mantra**

Use the mantra *Hum* this month. Chant it out loud or silently every day: while you're in the shower, before or after meditating, or at any other time that feels right to you.

◗ **Affirmation**

Say the following on the night of the Full Moon:

'As I express myself with love, life brings me all I need.'

Full Moon (or lunar eclipse) in your 4th House

(Also known as your Home and Family Zone)

◗ **In the coming two weeks…**

Pay attention to your family's needs, and to your own needs for personal space and private time.

◗ **Emotion alert!**

This Full Moon can bring up intense feelings about your family – bless them.

◗ **Messages**

Working like a dog to achieve your personal goals sounds like a very good thing, but there's a time and a place for everything. And at the time of your 4th House Full Moon, you're in a cycle when the planets (and the Sun and the Moon in particular) are suggesting that you need to find a balance between your outer aims and goals and your inner needs.

Perhaps your family needs you to spend more time with them. Or perhaps you just need some time with nothing on your mind. Take a look at your family relationships and ascertain if everything is running as smoothly as you'd like. If not, this is the time to pour some energy into that part of your life.

◗ Release any issues you have about…

Your personal life/home/family. Issues to do with your family can come up now, so be ready. Don't dread this, though: rather, see it as a chance to sort out any outstanding upsets. Our family members are people with whom we have a very karmic connection and any issues that come up do so to help us evolve.

The Full Moon here can also be a time when we make changes to where we live. If you're not sure about the best way forwards regarding your home, or *where* you call home, meditate on it and ask your Archangels, Goddesses and guides for direction. Issues and projects connected to the home can be resolved now.

◗ A tug-of-war may arise between…

What you want to achieve in your life professionally, and what you're required to do at home.

◗ Find a balance between…

Your personal life and your career. Maybe you're a driven person who forgets to have a personal life and neglects your partner/friends while working long hours, or perhaps you're a family type who knows you have more to offer the world; either way, this is your time to strike a balance. Ambition and family work well together: Success can allow you to spoil your loved ones, and your desire to provide for your family can inspire ambition.

◗ Forgive…

Yourself for any upsets you've had with family or flatmates. Make your home a peaceful sanctuary.

◗ Be grateful

Make your gratitude list.

◗ Mantra

Your mantra this Full Moon is *Om*. Chant it out loud or silently every day: while you're in the shower, before or after meditating, or at any other time that feels right to you.

◗ Affirmation

Say the following on the night of the Full Moon:

'I am safe and secure.'

Full Moon (or lunar eclipse) in your 5th House

(Also known as your Kids, Romance and Creativity Zone)

◗ In the coming two weeks…

Check whether you're having enough fun – fun is good for us.

◗ Emotion alert!

The Full Moon can bring up intense feelings about an issue to do with a child (your own or someone else's), your love life, or a creative project you're working on.

◗ Messages

There's usually a whole lot of emotion going on in your chart and your life at the time of the Full Moon in your 5th House of self-expression. You can be pouring your heart out – perhaps because you're sad, or maybe just because you have a lot of emotions to download.

For some of us, it's about the joy that a child (our own or someone else's) brings. And for others, it's about pouring emotion into a creative project we're working on. And while this is going on, you need to find a balance between your Self and your friends – don't neglect them totally. This is your challenge for the coming month.

◗ Release any issues you have about…

Allowing yourself some time off. The past few weeks may well have seen you working very hard, but now you may feel put upon by the need to look after your friends. Turn that around if you can and make this a very sociable time in which the person having the most fun is you.

An issue related to a child (your own or someone else's) can come to a peak now, hopefully for resolution in a way that makes everyone happy. If you have a creative project on the boil, it's a very good time to complete the latest stage or even finish it off altogether.

◗ A tug-of-war may arise between…

What your friends need and what you need for yourself. Self-expression is a focus. As are kids and creative projects.

◗ Find a balance between…

How much you cater to the needs of the groups and social circles to which you belong, versus how often *you* are taking centre stage – being yourself, speaking up, and letting the world know what you have to offer. It's safe to be with lots of people, doing what they do, but this is the time to show the world who *you* are. If a love affair ends now, it's doing so at the right time. One that starts now could be a very feelings-filled relationship that may even wax and wane with the Moon.

◗ Forgive…

Anyone who drags you down; yourself for any time you felt you weren't a great parent, or any time you took life too seriously.

◗ Be grateful

Make your gratitude list.

◗ Mantra

Use the mantra *Vam* this month. Chant it out loud or silently every day: while you're in the shower, before or after meditating, or at any other time that feels right to you.

◗ Affirmation

Say the following on the night of the Full Moon:

'I am a creative being!'

Full Moon (or lunar eclipse) in your 6th House

(Also known as your Daily Work and Health Zone)

◗ In the coming two weeks…

Find a way to bring peace into your life.

◗ Emotion alert!

This Full Moon can bring up intense feelings about what you do every day to earn a living. It can also herald fears about health (which may well be totally unfounded).

Messages

If you're one of the 'lucky ones' – i.e. you've been working on yourself – this is the Full Moon when you see yourself for who you *really* are. You therefore see your good points as well as your flaws – and you decide to do something about your flaws.

This is all about the daily life you lead. Are you living in a healthy fashion? Are you getting out and about to exercise? Have you long ago given up bad habits such as smoking and partying too much? If not, then this Full Moon is your annual chance to start again when it comes to taking care of yourself: body, mind and spirit. Routines are your friend at this Full Moon. At work, go slow and steady.

Release any issues you have about...

Habits that you need to break. This part of your chart is concerned with the daily rhythms of your life. If you're not happy with the way you're doing things – with the way your life is going along, with your morning or evening routines – this is the Full Moon to tune in to, to let go of the old ways and start to do them differently.

In particular, any unhealthy or even toxic habits should be released now: be it not drinking enough water, or drinking too much alcohol, or not doing enough exercise, or eating too much or not eating enough. Our daily habits impact our health and your 6th House is about habits and health. Look after your habits and your health should take care of itself.

A tug-of-war may arise between...

Your need to deal with the real world and do your duty, and your need to find some peaceful time out.

Find a balance between...

Your daily grind and the mysterious cosmos. Yes, you read that right. Most of us have a daily grind of some kind – things we need to do, responsibilities we have to take care of, duties we can't avoid – and then there's bliss, peace, time out, meditation, contemplation and the Great Void or the Gap: the mysterious 'place' in the Universe where we can just 'be'. Introducing a daily meditation or yoga practice can really help with balancing things up at the time of the Full Moon in the 6th House. In fact, it's highly recommended.

◗ Forgive…

The people you see every day who annoy you in little ways – quite possibly in much the same way that you niggle them. Forgive yourself for any unhealthy habits, make some changes, and move on.

◗ Be grateful

Make your gratitude list.

◗ Mantra

Use the mantra *Hum* this month. Chant it out loud or silently every day: while you're in the shower, before or after meditating, or at any other time that feels right to you.

◗ Affirmation

Say the following on the night of the Full Moon:

'I am in perfect health!'

Full Moon (or lunar eclipse) in your 7th House

(Also known as your Love Zone)

◗ In the coming two weeks…

Expect relationship issues to come to the fore.

◗ Emotion alert!

This Full Moon can bring up intense feelings about your love life.

◗ Messages

This Full Moon suggests it's time for *you* to step aside a little. It's time to invest some emotional energy into your other half (your marriage partner, or significant other) or into other people in your life (a business partner, a friend or even an adversary). Me, me, me is fine at the right time, but now it should be all about someone else.

At the very least, there should be a balance if someone else needs your attention. The Full Moon can also bring closures, so if you're in a friendship or a relationship that's ending now, you can proceed, knowing that you're finishing things up at exactly the right time, celestially speaking.

◗ Release any issues you have about...

Love and relationships. This can mean your present romantic situation, or one from the past. The whole point of relationships, on a karmic level, seems to be about us mere mortals learning lessons through other people. Someone who pushes our buttons is going to teach us a lot more about ourselves, and how to handle ourselves, than someone who doesn't.

That's why so many wonderful relationships are quite tense at times. That's the result of two souls evolving and learning to love though the tough times. The Full Moon in the 7th House can also be a time when we decide to sever ties on a relationship that's reached its 'use by' date, and that's okay too. Some people come to us for a reason or a season, as the saying goes.

◗ A tug-of-war may arise between...

What you need and what your partner or boss or best friend or other VIP needs.

◗ Find a balance between...

Thinking of yourself and thinking of someone else. The emotional Full Moon in your 7th House puts the spotlight on how you feel about someone important to you. This is also a very good time to practise your negotiating and compromising skills. Whether the relationship in question is with your lover, your partner, your ex, a business partner or an adversary, see what you can do to find common ground and you'll have milked the best of this Full Moon.

◗ Forgive...

Anyone and everyone who isn't you, and then forgive yourself for any relationship 'mistakes' you think you've made. (Believe it or not, there really is no such thing as a mistake: Everything happens for a reason and everything is perfect and just as it should be.)

◗ Be grateful

Make your gratitude list.

◗ Mantra

Use the mantra *Yum* this month. Chant it out loud or silently every day: while you're in the shower, before or after meditating, or at any other time that feels right to you.

◗ Affirmation

Say the following on the night of the Full Moon:

'I am loved, I am loving, I am lovable!'

Full Moon (or lunar eclipse) in your 8th House

(Also known as your Sex and Shared Finances Zone)

◗ In the coming two weeks...

Sort out your feelings about sex and money.

◗ Emotion alert!

This Full Moon can bring up intense feelings about your sex life and your finances.

◗ Messages

This Full Moon is all about finding a balance between what you give in life and what you take. If you know you've been doing too much of either, this Full Moon is most certainly the time to redress the balance. The problem is that when we give too much but don't know how to take, we actually mess with the natural laws that govern free flow. How can the Universe send you an abundant stream of good things if you're not receiving them without a fight?

This Full Moon also heralds a very good period to attend to practical financial matters, such as paying off debts and settling personal bills. It's also very good for investing some emotion in the boudoir.

◗ Release any issues you have about...

Anything that's holding you back or bogging you down or stopping you from living the life that you want. The 8th House is all about death and rebirth, reinvention and transformation. It can be a scary part of the chart: after all, it's where death and taxes reside – and those subjects can come up when this part of your chart is being triggered.

But don't worry. The Full Moon happens here once a year (at least) and you're certainly not likely to have to deal with the heaviest aspects of it annually. Rather, look at the Full Moon here as a chance to transform as a person. It's also about cash: more about that below.

◗ A tug-of-war may arise between…

Your money and where your money meets someone else's.

◗ Find a balance between…

How much you think you're worth and how much you're actually being remunerated for your efforts at work. It's about self-worth versus the worth someone else puts on you. It's also about being your own boss financially versus depending on others to pay you – your salary, your debts, anything.

Financial windfalls and inheritances aren't out of the question when this part of your chart is active. This part is also about sex, and issues around sex and sexuality can come up. This is good because it's the right time to deal with them and move on.

◗ Forgive…

Anyone you feel has overstepped the mark, hurt you or broken a taboo. Also forgive yourself for any problems you've had with money that you blame yourself for.

◗ Be grateful

Make your gratitude list.

◗ Mantra

Vam is the mantra for this Full Moon. Chant it out loud or silently every day: while you're in the shower, before or after meditating, or at any other time that feels right to you.

Affirmation

Say the following on the night of the Full Moon:

'I shed my past and I evolve!'

Full Moon (or lunar eclipse) in your 9th House

(Also known as your 'Big Picture' Zone)

In the coming two weeks...

Deal with worries you have connected to study, travel and the Great Cosmic Quest.

Emotion alert!

This Full Moon can bring up intense feelings about where you're going: your life philosophies.

Messages

Personal growth, religion, philosophy, publishing, the internet, travel and study – these are just some of the subjects looming large for you when the Full Moon takes place in your 9th House. Be honest with yourself: Have you been fussing too much over the details of your latest problems or tasks? Sometimes, that's just a delay tactic and we need to take a step back and look at the big picture of where we are and where we want to be.

Are your life and your mind expanding or narrowing? If you've stopped being adventurous, then you only have yourself to blame. This is a great time to try something that lies beyond your usual realm of the everyday.

Release any issues you have about...

The grass being greener. The Full Moon here means it's time for you to see the bigger picture of your life. You may be having a crisis and wondering whether this is all there is. Take a moment to see the broader vista. Hopefully doing so will prompt you to count your blessings.

This is also a time for you to think about whether you want to get away from it all or stay right where you are. Will the grass be greener if you go away? If you're staying at home, someone abroad could also have your attention. There's no way of telling. Also at this time, legal issues can resolve themselves or at least come to the fore.

◗ A tug-of-war may arise between...

Being here and wanting to be there. Being torn between home and away. Small ideas versus big ideas.

◗ Find a balance between...

Your thoughts and your faith. This is a chance for you to let go of fear and limiting ideas and to accept the concept of a power bigger than all of us out in the Great Unknown. If you're going through a 'dark night of the soul' at the time of your 9th House New Moon, at least take solace in the fact that your timing is perfect, cosmically speaking. This is a chance for you to grow spiritually and to expand your understanding of the world around you. Open yourself up to new ideas.

◗ Forgive...

People who are narrow-minded, or yourself if you've been narrow-minded.

◗ Be grateful

Make your gratitude list.

◗ Mantra

This month's mantra is *Ah*. Chant it out loud or silently every day: while you're in the shower, before or after meditating, or at any other time that feels right to you.

◗ Affirmation

Say the following on the night of the Full Moon:

'I know I am blessed!'

Full Moon (or lunar eclipse) in your 10th House

(Also known as your Career Zone)

◗ In the coming two weeks...

Sort out issues related to your work.

◗ Emotion alert!

The Full Moon can bring up intense feelings about your career and professional trajectory.

◗ Messages

If you've been hiding yourself away and generally keeping a low profile, watch out. The skies are suggesting rather loudly that it's time for you to step out of the shadows and back into the limelight. As tempting as it might be to slouch around at home, the Full Moon in your 10th House is telling you it's time to invest some emotional energy in your professional life.

Even if your work has been the source of annoyance lately, don't give up. For some, a work situation or project comes to an end now. Don't panic. Remember, the Universe abhors a vacuum and something new will come in to take its place soon enough.

How committed are you to your goals? This can be your time to shine at work. When the Full Moon takes place in your 10th House, aka your Career Zone, it's as though you're being pushed into the spotlight professionally, ready or not. For some of us it will be because a big work project is coming to fruition. Hopefully you'll receive accolades for all your hard work.

On the other hand, if a project or a job is coming to an end now, there's at least consolation in the fact that it's happening in Divine timing. This is a good time to ask yourself how you feel about you career. Where do you want to go next with it?

◗ Release any issues you have about...

Your workload and how it impacts your home life.

◗ A tug-of-war may arise between...

Your duties at home, and all that you need to do to get ahead in your career.

◗ Find a balance between...

Who you are inside versus who you are out in the world – as someone who does or doesn't seek to 'achieve'. As with the Full Moon in the 4th House, this lunation asks you to find a work/life balance. There could be tensions or demands at home that are affecting your ability to function at peak levels at work.

Or work dramas could be keeping you from living a rich personal life. Whatever the case, this is the second chance you have in this 12-month cycle to find a balance. For some, recognition comes now; for others, it becomes clear that more emotional investment is needed professionally.

◗ Forgive...

Anyone you feel has done you wrong professionally; and yourself for any untoward behaviour at work, ever.

◗ Be grateful

Make your gratitude list.

◗ Mantra

Use the mantra *Lam* this month. Chant it out loud or silently every day – in the shower, before or after meditating, or at any other time that feels right to you

◗ Affirmation

Say the following on the night of the Full Moon:

'I have a perfect work, in a perfect way;
I give a perfect service, for perfect pay!'

(This perfect affirmation comes from the book *The Game of Life and How to Play It*, which was written by metaphysician Florence Scovel Shinn in 1925. Her books are *so* worth reading.)

Full Moon (or lunar eclipse) in your 11th House

(Also known as your Friends Zone)

◗ In the coming two weeks…

Deal with any upsets with friends.

◗ Emotion alert!

The Full Moon can bring up intense feelings about friendships, and unfulfilled dreams.

◗ Messages

It's tempting to focus on yourself and your own pleasures. Perhaps you're a creative type who loves to express yourself. And why not? After all, life is for living and having fun. However, this month's

Full Moon in your 11th House is reminding you that you need to find a balance between indulging in a bit of what you fancy and remembering that the people in your life also need attention from you. Whatever you do now for someone else, you'll get extra karmic Brownie points. This also makes the coming month good for networking.

What are you dreaming of? And do you know anyone who can help you get it? The Full Moon here casts a warm and gentle light on your wishes. Are they working for you? Are you getting what you're dreaming of? And if not, why do you think that is? It's a strange but true fact that sometimes we just know we're not going to get what we're paying lip service to wishing for. Sometimes we know on an intuitive level that something is never going to happen. Or perhaps we no longer want what we once desired. The Full Moon in your 11th House is the ideal time to release anything like this into the ether.

This part of your chart is also, crucially, about friends and networks. How are you with your friends now? Are you happy with them? Would you like to make new friends? Issues related to friends can arise at this time. Breathe deep before you deal with them. A friendship that ends at this Full Moon is definitely ending at the right cosmic time.

◗ Release any issues you have about…

What you've been wishing for. Are there dreams that don't seem to manifest, or friendships that are troubling you?

◗ A tug-of-war may arise between…

Who you are, versus who your friends are.

◗ Find a balance between…

What you need for yourself versus what you need to do for, and give to, your friends. The 11th House is about the clubs, groups and social networks you belong to. When the Full Moon falls here, chances are you'll have at least one friendship that needs your attention.

Are you pulling your weight within your group of friends, or does someone have cause for complaint? Or is it you who feels someone else could be a better friend? The Full Moon here reminds you that you have to balance your own needs with those of your social circles, networks and groups.

◗ Forgive...

Any friend who hurt you, at any point in your life; and yourself for whatever you feel you did or didn't do in relation to that friendship.

◗ Be grateful

Make your gratitude list.

◗ Mantra

Use the mantra *Om* this Full Moon. Chant it out loud or silently every day – in the shower, before or after meditating, or at any other time that feels right to you.

◗ Affirmation

Say the following on the night of the Full Moon:

'I am a great friend and I attract great friends!'

And/or

'My dreams and wishes are now manifesting!'

Full Moon (or lunar eclipse) in your 12th House

(Also known as your Secrets Zone)

◗ In the coming two weeks…

Take time out.

◗ Emotion alert!

This Full Moon can bring up intense feelings about your secret self.

◗ Messages

Life has probably felt very busy recently and no one can blame you for wanting to take some time out. The Full Moon in your 12th House is going to allow you to do just that. For many people, this Full Moon comes at a time when they're feeling a little bit down in the dumps, but the fact is, they're likely just exhausted after the efforts of keeping up with the demands of daily life. Take some time out. Meditate or practise yoga. You need to strike a balance between working and taking time out.

The worst thing about a 12th House Full Moon is that it forces you to look at where you may have been sabotaging yourself with your own behaviour. The best thing about a 12th House Full Moon is that it forces you to look at where you may have been sabotaging yourself with your own behaviour. Get it?

The 12th House is unfortunately known as the House of Self-Undoing. We all have a 12th House and we all have parts of ourselves that are indeed our own worst enemy. The good news is that when the Full Moon takes place in this part of your chart, it's a wonderful chance to identify that behaviour – to see it for what it is and let it go.

◗ Release any issues you have about...

Things you don't like to talk about. Forgive other people for anything they've done to you, and forgive yourself for anything you've done to yourself or anyone else – overtly or covertly.

◗ A tug-of-war may arise between...

The things you have to do every day to keep life ticking over and your need for inner peace.

◗ Find a balance between...

Your daily life as a functioning human being and that secret side of you that's mysterious, delicate and perhaps even a bit dark. For some it's what we think we should hide and for others it's what others (probably parents) have told us we should hide. This Full Moon can bring up some pretty intense feelings, whether we like it or not.

We may even find ourselves apologizing – because this is the House of Self-Undoing, and not expressing how we feel is a wonderful way to self-undo or self-sabotage. The month when you have your personal, annual Full Moon in the 12th House is the ideal time to go on a retreat, if that appeals to you. It's a time to do inner work and even to explore your spirituality. Sometimes, this Full Moon will bring or reveal a big secret. Go easy on yourself at this time of the year: it's one of the most emotionally intense Full Moons. The next one will be easier.

◗ Forgive...

Yourself for anything you feel ashamed of. Understand that there's nothing to be ashamed of: we're all growing. Forgive anyone else who has ever hurt you.

◗ Be grateful

Make your gratitude list.

◗ Mantra

Use the mantra *Ah* this month. Chant it out loud or silently every day – in the shower, before or after meditating, or at any other time that feels right to you.

◗ Affirmation

Say the following on the night of the Full Moon:

'It's okay to have quality "me" time.'

Summary

You now have all the information you need to work with the Full Moon. In this section you learned:

- Why the Full Moon is ideal for forgiving, and why forgiveness is crucial to manifesting.
- Why gratitude is so important, and how it replaces the negativity released under the Full Moon.
- The meaning of the Full Moon through all 12 signs.
- The meaning of the Full Moon through all 12 Houses.

FAQs: the Full Moon

◗ What if I don't want to forgive someone?

A reader once wrote to me to say that she didn't want to forgive her ex-husband, who had abused her. That was understandable in some ways; however, it wasn't helping her to move on. The point is that forgiving someone doesn't make what they did right. Rather, it releases you from it, so you can get on with the next stage in your life. Otherwise, in some way, that person from your past is still in your present and continues to have a hold on you.

◗ Can I make wishes at the Full Moon?

Yes, you can make wishes at the both the New and Full Moons. However, in theory, the Full Moon is the peak of the cycle and the days that follow are about relaxing and letting go. Ideally if you make your wishes at the time of the New Moon then the two weeks that follow (leading up to the Full Moon) are more dynamic and all about you working hard to make your dreams come true. However, I'm of the belief that it's better to wish at the Full Moon than not to get clear on your wishes at all.

◗ What if a Full Moon happens on my birthday?

A Full Moon, or Full Moon eclipse, on your birthday suggests a year ahead that will be something of a turning point. It's time to find a balance, possibly between you and how much time you're giving to others. Emotions need to be dealt with. It's a year to be especially conscious of how well you handle your feelings.

PART IV

Live Consciously with the Moon

Knowing where the Moon is every day can guide you. If you decide to work with the Moon and live consciously, there are certain activities and areas of life that you're better off doing (or not doing) or exploring at certain times.

CHAPTER 9

Where Is the Daily Moon?

We've looked at New Moons and Full Moons but what about the Daily Moon? Does that count? Most definitely.

Here's a quick recap: the New Moon happens when the Sun and the Moon are in the same place at the same time, and the Full Moon is when the Sun and the Moon are on opposite sides of the zodiac. And the Daily Moon? That's where the Moon is on any given day. Remember, the Moon moves through all 12 signs and all 12 Houses of your chart once a month.

Just visit my site – yasminboland.com – to find out where the Moon is every day. Alternatively, you can follow me online or download an astrology app.

Once you know where the Moon is on a particular day, ask yourself whether it's in a Fire, Earth, Air or Water sign: here's how to find out:

- **Fire:** Aries, Leo and Sagittarius
- **Earth:** Taurus, Virgo and Capricorn
- **Air:** Gemini, Libra and Aquarius
- **Water:** Cancer, Scorpio and Pisces

Next you need to know that:

- **Fire** = fiery/impulsive/passionate

- **Earth** = grounded/practical/stable
- **Air** = chatty/flighty/intellectual
- **Water** = emotional/psychic/mysterious

A guide to the Daily Moon in each sign

Therefore, the Moon – the so-called Queen of Emotions – in a fiery Fire sign means more fiery emotions. It's that simple. In a snip, you get a flavour of the day. And remember, a shift in the zodiac sign that the Moon is in means a shift in the mood. And in case you're wondering, the Moon changes signs at the same time all over the world.

After that it's simply a matter of applying what you know about a sign to the Moon. For example, the Aries energy for the Daily Moon is very similar to the energy of the Aries New Moon. The 'Moon Days' guide below describes the energies of the Daily Moon in each of the 12 signs of the zodiac and describes what each day is good for – and not so good for.

Daily Moon in Aries ♈

Emotions can run high when the Moon is in Aries – after all, Aries is ruled by the angry war planet Mars. So be careful if you're very Moon-tuned and find yourself in the middle of an argument. Take a few deep breaths and remind yourself that the Aries Moon is no excuse to lose your hard-earned cool. It's far better to use the Aries energy to Get Things Done. Aries Moon Days are filled with impulsive energy, and it's easy to feel quite driven. We may as well channel that energy into something constructive, right? It's also a time when enthusiasm flows. Try not to take offence too easily today. This is also a seriously good day for meditation, as we all need that extra injection of Zen when the Moon is in Aries.

◗ **Good for…**

Racing through the day.

◗ **Not so good for…**

Quiet introspection.

◗ **Do…**

Go faster.

◗ **Don't…**

Pick a fight.

Daily Moon in Taurus ♉

This is a lovely Moon sign – the Moon and Taurus go really well together. They both have a bit of a 'food' thing going on: the Moon rules food and Taurus loves food. This is a sensual and relaxing Moon placement so try not to have anything too jarring to do. Having a massage or lazing around all day in bed with your lover/cat/a cup of tea is ideal. This is a No Rush day.

That said, if you do have a lot to achieve today, the slow and steady plod of Taurus will aid and abet you. If you're aiming to increase your cash flow, the abundant Taurus Moon makes it a very good time to work on your visualizations and plans.

◗ **Good for…**

Relaxing and canoodling, eating and basking.

◗ **Not so good for…**

Doing unpleasant tasks.

◗ Do…

Indulge your senses and enjoy some creature comforts.

◗ Don't…

Be stubborn.

Daily Moon in Gemini ♊

The day can seem to go very fast, because the Moon is in the quicksilver sign of Gemini. This can be a good thing if you're not already overworked, but a tad confusing if you've a lot on your plate. Certainly it's a busy day. This might sound like the Aries Daily Moon (*see page 194*), but it's different: Aries Moon Days are about action, while the Gemini Moon is more about mental energy – talking to lots of people and non-stop moving about.

If you have a presentation to give today, you have the stars (or rather the Moon) on your side. Similarly, a Gemini Moon Day is a great time to hold a social gathering (aka a party) because everyone is going to be extra chatty, which oils the social wheels. Conversations today can make sense of a lot of things. It's a day to be inquisitive.

◗ Good for…

Socializing, thinking, reading, talking – and generally taking your communications skills for a whirl.

◗ Not so good for…

Being totally Zen – there's too much to do and too many places to go.

◗ Do…

Call up your best pal, your siblings/parents and anyone else on your 'must call' list.

◗ Don't…

Keep gabbing away on social media until you embarrass yourself. You'll know when to stop, so do it.

Daily Moon in Cancer ♋

After the carry-on of the past few days, the world breathes a sigh of relief as the Moon moves into home-loving Cancer. This is a day to retreat to the bosom of your family, or at least to be at home. The vibe mellows and suddenly, domesticity beckons. It's a day to feather your nest.

Sort out your home if it's in a bit of a mess. Clear up, clean up and do the washing. Have friends or family over to enjoy a good meal. (Cancer loves food!) If you find yourself giving in to the slightly insecure Cancer vibe, have a word with yourself. A Cancer Moon Day is a wonderful time to work on your doubts and fears. Don't scuttle away under a rock. Work out what's worrying you. This is also a good day to show someone your soft underbelly. Don't be too hard-headed.

◗ Good for…

Baking, staying in and getting cosy. Spending time with loved ones. Coming up with a dynamic plan: the Cancer energy is also very entrepreneurial.

◗ Not so good for…

Being detached, aloof and unemotional.

◗ Do…

Spend time with kids you adore; be hospitable; take time out.

◗ Don't…

Drag yourself to any place you don't feel like going, unless you totally have to.

Daily Moon in Leo ♌

It's time to show off a little! Leo is the showstopper sign of the zodiac and when the Moon makes Her monthly trek through Leo, you can be sure someone somewhere is turning heads. If you need to do something with confidence, a Leo Moon Day is a great place to start.

The Leo Moon is also very creative and even artistic. It's a day to show the world 'what you've got'. Don't hide your light under a bushel on a Leo Moon Day: that would be a total waste of the energies. Any showbiz-related razzamatazz is very well 'starred' (Mooned) today, too. So tune in to the Leo Moon, and organize something fun to do.

◗ Good for…

Partying, wearing lampshades, making 'em laugh, being awesome.

◗ Not so good for…

Feeling like a shrinking violet.

◗ Do…

Put your best foot forward.

◗ Don't…

Fake humility – no one will fall for it today anyway.

Daily Moon in Virgo ♍

Okay, so maybe it's time to settle down a little after two and a bit days of the Leo madness. The Virgo Moon puts on its monocle, makes sure all the things on its desk are present and correct, and starts to do whatever it has to in order to keep life ticking over as it's meant to. The Virgo Moon is a wonderful day to take stock, crunch the numbers and get a pretty good idea of where you are in life.

Where would you like to operate more efficiently? Or generally function better? A Virgo Moon Day is ideal for starting that up. It's also a very good day to think about your diet and general health regimes. If you feel you need treatment of some kind, complementary medicine is a good place to start (but do see a GP if you have pain that persists).

◗ Good for...

Releasing addictions, getting your life in order, creating new routines.

◗ Not so good for...

Going wild, being reckless, or doing other stupid stuff (although kinkiness with your beloved can work).

◗ Do...

Be helpful.

◗ Don't...

Be too critical.

Daily Moon in Libra ♎

This is sort of the equivalent of the Moon in the 7th House. And if Jupiter is aligned with Mars? Whoosh! Libra is the sign of partnership and relationships, so when the Moon is in this sign, it's a wonderful time to turn your mind to matters romantic. And also to business matters involving partnerships. Are you giving and taking in equal amounts? Do you need to make your move on someone you have your eye on?

It's also a good day to make peace with an ex you've loved and lost. Libra loves to negotiate, too, so if you have a personal or professional matter on which you'd like to reach agreement, all things being equal – i.e. ego Saturn not clashing with Pluto or some such thing – this is the right day to start the conversation. It's also basically just a great day for love, so shower the people you love with love. Wining and dining is also highly recommended.

◗ Good for…

Romance and partnerships of all kinds.

◗ Not so good for…

Being alone.

◗ Do…

Be ready to come to an agreement.

◗ Don't…

Let your head rule your heart.

Daily Moon in Scorpio ♏

Here's the thing: Scorpio is a wonderful sign and we all have Scorpio somewhere in our chart, but it's also very much a part of our shadow side. And when the Moon moves through Scorpio, it does take on some of this Scorpionic energy, which, like the Scorpion itself, has a sting. So mind how you go on a Scorpio Moon Day.

Tread carefully with anyone known to have a short fuse or a mean streak. And if you know you have a bit of a nasty sting in your own tail, do your meditations today. It's a day when minor upsets and petty jealousies can crop up to remind us we're humans on the evolutionary trail. The good news about Scorpio is that it's a transformational energy, so used correctly, a Scorpio Moon Day can actually have a major impact, be it material or physical or psychological.

◗ Good for…

Investigating a mystery, getting to the bottom of something, being a tad obsessive about someone you adore.

◗ Not so good for…

Being way too obsessive, developing bad habits or snooping.

◗ Do…

Lighten up.

◗ Don't…

Give in to the shadow.

Daily Moon in Sagittarius ♐

If you fancy letting off some steam and overindulging yourself, you've read this on the right day. A Sagittarius Moon Day is the one for taking things as far as you can. The energy is connected to the planet Jupiter, who loves excess and pretty much always overdoes it. Of course, all this 'have your cake and eat it too' can come at a cost. Be careful not to throw caution to the wind totally today. Being adventurous is one thing but being reckless is another.

This is also a great day to dream about the amazing book you want to publish (or to write that book), or to put your mind to ideas of travel or study. It's also a good time to see the big picture – doing this can really help us get things into perspective and move us into that all-important state of gratitude from which all good things come.

◗ Good for…

Having fun, rolling the dice, taking a chance, taking the first step, being adventurous.

◗ Not so good for…

Reining things in, dampening your enthusiasm, limiting yourself.

◗ Do…

Go for it – fortune favours Sagittarius.

◗ Don't…

Play it cautious.

Daily Moon in Capricorn ♑

Need to get yourself together? Get your head in order? Make a plan? Then a Capricorn Moon Day has your back. Capricorn is the most ordered and ambitious of the signs so when the Moon is here, being sensible and strategic is the order of the day. It's a wonderful time to get your life back on track. Think about where you've been, where you want to go and what kind of mark you want to leave on the world.

It's a day when relationships with bosses, or your position as a boss, could come to the fore. Behaving maturely and thinking long-term are the keys to success now. Be smart, but don't be too serious. Work out your goals for the months ahead (it's a good day to do your month-ahead plan), but don't let all this squeeze the joy out.

◗ Good for...

Achieving career goals.

◗ Not so good for...

Lounging around.

◗ Do...

Use the day to get yourself back on the path that will take you towards your idea of success.

◗ Don't...

Forget to have some fun.

Daily Moon in Aquarius ♒

Aquarius Moon Days have a slightly nerve-jangling quality. (Or is that just me?) It's as though we all need to start to be a tad more progressive and think about the future. Aquarius is all about modernization and progress. And when the Moon is in Aquarius, the status quo might very well go. It's a great day to rebel and be non-conformist, too. Aquarius is an energy that likes to live outside the box.

So if you're a bit like that, you should find that the Universe (or rather the Moon) supports you in being your wackiest, best self. It's also a wonderful day to get together with friends, and if it's for a charitable cause, so much the better. Aquarius loves to do good things for the world, and to do those things with as many people as possible. Nothing charitable to do? It's still a good day for a gathering.

◗ Good for…

Making wishes.

◗ Not so good for…

Doing things the old-fashioned way; trying to halt progress.

◗ Do…

Be fashion-forward and forward-thinking and, well, just *forward.*

◗ Don't…

Be surprised if you're too frank and people take offence.

Daily Moon in Pisces ♓

On a good Pisces Moon Day, life can feel dreamy and romantic. It's a day when one hour melts into the next and no one seems in too much of a rush for anything. Poetry can be written and read. Meditations go deeper. Soulmates can appear, or unite or reunite. The word 'soulful' gets put to good use.

What's not to like about a Pisces Moon Day? Well, addictions might be an issue for some of us. Self-pity, a sense of being lost, and of being a martyr, happen more readily on a Pisces Moon Day. But it's a balance: Just as a Pisces Moon Day can be about altered states reached with drugs and alcohol, it can also be about getting into an altered state by doing a spiritual practice that connects you to the Divine. Or even better, because of being with someone who makes you feel like you've seen God/dess.

◗ **Good for…**

Swimming, dreaming, bathing.

◗ **Not so good for…**

Rigorous mental or physical work, arguments, being down to earth.

◗ **Do…**

Dream a little or big dream.

◗ **Don't…**

Expect it to come true without some concrete follow-through.

CHAPTER 10

Up Close and Personal with the Daily Moon

Now we're going to look at the movement of the Daily Moon through the Houses. It has to be said that this won't have a massive impact on your life, as the Moon moves so fast and Her effects are so fleeting. However, as you learn about astrology, it can be a wonderful thing to track the Moon's movements around your chart.

Moreover, if you decide to work with the Moon and live consciously, it's recommended that you do particular things as the Moon makes Her way through all 12 Houses of your chart over the course of a month.

To work out where the Moon is in your chart, first find out which sign She is in. You can find that every day on the home page of my site – yasminboland.com. Then refer to the table on pages 84–85.

A guide to the Daily Moon in each House

The following guide offers some ideas about how to work with the Daily Moon as it moves through your chart:

Daily Moon in your 1st House

This is a day to go out and show the world what your mama gave you. The emphasis is on how you look, and if you're not too happy with that state of affairs, this is the time of the month to give yourself a makeover – be it a new hairstyle or some new clothes. Also be aware that the Moon is all about feelings, and as She passes through this 'front door' of your chart (because that's what the 1st House is), you could be way more emotional than usual.

That's okay: We all have to deal with our feelings every now and then, and the Moon in the 1st House is an exceedingly good time to do so. Also be aware that the Moon here exacerbates your rising sign. So if you have a really outgoing rising sign, such as Aries or Leo, you could be more 'out there' than usual. On the contrary, more timid types, such as Virgos and Cancerians, may want to keep a lower profile.

Daily Moon in your 2nd House

Feelings about money can come up today. Cash, property and possessions are all subjects on the lunar chart and up for discussion. If you have to deal with something like that, do be careful not to allow your emotions to get the better of you. If you find yourself feeling discombobulated about your finances, be honest with yourself about where this is coming from.

Is there something you can do to make yourself feel better about your cash flow (such as spending less, saving more, seeing a financial advisor or talking to your personal banker)? Issues related to self-esteem can arise on a Daily Moon in the 2nd House day too. All the better for you to make peace with your own magnificence as you boldly continue through life.

Daily Moon in your 3rd House

I hope you like your conversations meaningful and full of feelings, because that's what you're likely to get today as the Moon moves through your 3rd House of communications. It's potentially a rather busy day for you as well, with lots of errands to run and people to see. Do be ready to really engage with people.

There will be people around today who very much want to pour their heart out to you – or maybe it's you who's doing that to them. Brothers and sisters, and interactions with neighbours, can feature today, too. Sometimes these will concern seemingly unimportant things, but if you need to, the Moon here can help you sort out an issue. Just stay calm as you talk from your heart. This is also a good day for writing a heartfelt letter or email.

Daily Moon in your 4th House

If you can spend the day at home, do it. The Moon is oh so at home in this part of your chart, which is down the bottom of the zodiac circle and sort of hidden away and very private. So time spent alone can be a very good thing. As can time spent with friends and family, but preferably at home and preferably at *your* home.

The overriding energy today is about home and family and domestic issues, and doing things around the house – pottering. Cooking is also a great thing to do: feeding people, and generally nurturing them and yourself. The 4th House energy is also about you looking at how far you've come. Introspection is encouraged.

Daily Moon in your 5th House

It's time to shake off any melancholy and get back into society. The Moon is moving through your 5th House, which is the part of your chart where you like to have fun; where you party, holiday, do hobbies and generally have a good time. If you can, schedule in something like going out with friends, or doing something a little raucous. Enjoying yourself should be the order of the day.

This is a time to hang out with your kids, too, if you have them. Or with someone else's kids if you don't. Kids know how to enjoy themselves in a way that we adults tend to have forgotten. Connecting with little ones who know how to have a good belly laugh is one of the best ways to make the most of the Moon in your 5th House. Ditto doing something creative. Whatever gets your juices flowing will do. It's also a great Moon for romance, so if there's someone you love - or who floats your boat - around, connect with them! Take them out, or let them take you out. Feel those lovely feelings.

Daily Moon in your 6th House

The 6th House is the part of your chart where you worry less about what others can do for you and more about what you can do for others. How can you be of service? What do other people need and how can you help them to get it? Even if you think of yourself most of the time, when the Moon is in this part of your chart you have a chance to create some good karma for yourself by doing as you'd be done by without a thought for being paid back.

This is also a great time to think about your health. If you've departed from the straight and narrow, use the Moon in this part of your chart to recommit to a healthy lifestyle. The Moon here will support your decision. This can be a very productive time, during which you can get a lot done, so no slacking off. It's also a great day to tidy everything.

Daily Moon in your 7th House

Love and romance (oh, and enemies!) are the focus on the days when the Daily Moon is in your 7th House. It's time for you to connect with important other people, one on one. Talk to them, find out what they want, who they really are, and let them see the real you.

When the Moon is here, it's all about relating. This includes romantic relationships, so if you're married or attached, the Moon can bring up an issue that requires you to slow down and really see each other (something that's all too easy to avoid doing in this busy world). Feel the love, if it's there. If you're single, it's a great day to turn your mind to a possible new relationship, or to meet someone. The 7th House can also be about non-romantic partnerships such as a business relationship. It's a good day to shore up professional relationships.

Daily Moon in your 8th House

If you were ever to schedule in a time to have sex with your partner, then the day when the Moon is in their 8th House, or yours, is a very good choice. Admittedly, this would mean you only have sex twice a month at most, but if you're at the stage of scheduling it in, then twice a month is better than nothing, right? The 8th House is a mysterious place and sex sits well here.

The Moon through your 7th House hopefully brought you closer together, and now the Moon here allows you to go deeper with each other. Doesn't sound likely? This part of your chart is also about shared finances. In other words, where your money meets someone else's – such as in a salary, a loan or a debt. Issues related to these areas can come up now. Top tip: stay calm and deal with it. It's also a good day to do deep inner work on yourself.

Daily Moon in your 9th House

When the Moon moves through this part of your chart, it's your chance to escape. To get away from it all; to dream of another life, even. The Moon here reminds you that there are bigger vistas out there. A whole wide world, in fact – and if you can't go there on your own two feet, you can at least find ways to bring it to you.

That could be via talking to a well-travelled friend, or by eating out in an ethnic restaurant, or armchair travelling while watching an exotic TV show or film. The idea now is to expand your horizons and see the world outside your window. Because the 9th House also governs legal matters, sometimes they come up or are concluded at this time. Broaden your perspective today somehow. For some, travel or study will do the trick.

Daily Moon in your 10th House

What are your ambitions? What can you feasibly achieve right now and what do you hope to accomplish in the future? As the Moon moves through your 10th House, it's time to turn your mind to how you feel about your brilliant career. If it's going well, it can go even better at this time.

There could even be some kind of recognition coming your way. If your professional life isn't going too well right now though, the Moon in your 10th House is likely to bring up issues and emotions that you'll just have to face up to, if you want to live consciously and move towards your dreams. You may also have to deal with authority figures right now, or perhaps you're the one who is the 'superior'. If so, be nice! Sometimes what comes up is the chance to make your mark on the world. Or at least a hint about how to do that. Pay attention.

Daily Moon in your 11th House

It's time to get out and about with the people you like to hang out with the most. When the Moon moves through your 11th House, your friends are in focus, as are any groups you belong to – social networks, sports clubs, yoga classes and so on. It's where you're a part of a bigger group that you have potential for growth right now. Make sure you're giving as much as you're getting back.

It's also a time when you're more likely to enjoy being sociable. On top of that, chances are you've something extra to offer the group. If you need emotional support right now, with the Moon here, you're more than likely to get it. Women in particular could be flocking around you now. Also, your dreams and wishes may come into focus at this time. Do you still want what you used to want, and how are you going to get it?

Daily Moon in your 12th House

If you can, this is the time to retreat and withdraw from the world. The Moon has moved into the deepest and most private part of your chart and chances are you're going to want some time alone. Do everything you can to get it! You deserve it, you've undoubtedly earned it and you'll feel better for having it. Sometimes when the Moon triggers this part of your chart, the intrigue of the day is some kind of secret, or other 'hidden' thing.

Be aware that what's hidden now could come to light when the Moon crosses your ascendant (aka your rising sign) in a few days' time. The Moon in your 12th House is the ideal moment to look back over the past month and consider your actions and unconscious patterns or behaviour. Is there anything you'd like to change in the next cycle you're about to enter?

Summary

So now you have the information you need to work with the Daily Moon. In this section you learned that:

- Like the New and Full moons, the Daily Moon has a certain 'flavour' to it, depending on which sign it's in.

- The sign that the Daily Moon is in will lend a particular quality to the energies of the day.
- The House that the Daily Moon is in for you personally will influence the effect it has on you.

FAQs: the Daily Moon

And finally, here are some answers to common questions about the Daily Moon.

◗ Is the sign the Daily Moon is in on my birthday relevant?

Yes, in as much as astrologers will cast a chart for your year ahead on your birthday. That's known as your solar return chart. The sign that the Daily Moon is in on that chart (i.e. the sign it's in on your birthday) is the Moon sign that will influence you a lot in the 12 months after your birthday. Pay attention to it and then notice when the Moon is in that sign. How do you feel? There could be more emotional days for you, but also days of lovely feelings.

◗ Is there a Daily Moon that's especially good for love?

The Moon in Libra is especially good for love, since Libra is the sign of partnerships. However, the best way to work out your 'good love days' is to note when the Moon is triggering your 7th House, aka your Love Zone. First, you'll need to know your rising sign, which you can find at moonologybook.com/freechart.

Once you know that, you can find out the *ruler* of your Love Zone (*see table opposite*). When the Moon is in that sign, your Love Zone is being triggered and it's potentially a good day for love OR it's a day when feelings about important relationships will come up to be dealt with.

Which sign rules your 7th House, aka your Love Zone?			
♈	Aries or Aries rising	♎	Libra
♉	Taurus or Taurus rising	♏	Scorpio
♊	Gemini or Gemini rising	♐	Sagittarius
♋	Cancer or Cancer rising	♑	Capricorn
♌	Leo or Leo rising	♒	Aquarius
♍	Virgo or Virgo rising	♓	Pisces
♎	Libra or Libra rising	♈	Aries
♏	Scorpio or Scorpio rising	♉	Taurus
♐	Sagittarius or Sagittarius rising	♊	Gemini
♑	Capricorn or Capricorn rising	♋	Cancer
♒	Aquarius or Aquarius rising	♌	Leo
♓	Pisces or Pisces rising	♍	Virgo

◗ What if the Daily Moon is in my sign?

It means you're getting or you're about to get (in the coming two and a bit days) your personal New Moon. The Moon takes a month to go around the chart through all the signs. If you're a Virgo (i.e. your Sun is in Virgo) then when the Moon is in Virgo, we know that the Moon is going over the spot where the Sun was when you were born. Put the Sun and the Moon together in the same time and the same place and you get a New Moon. In this case, it's a personal New Moon made up of the Moon in the skies and your personal Sun. It's a time of renewal, but it can also be an emotional hot spot for you!

Which sign is [illegible] your Daily Moon [illegible]

♈	Aries [illegible]	♎	Libra
♉	Taurus [illegible]	♏	Scorpio
♊	Gemini [illegible]	♐	Sagittarius
♋	Cancer [illegible]	♑	Capricorn
♌	[illegible]	♒	[illegible]
♍	[illegible]	♓	[illegible]
♎	[illegible]	♈	[illegible]
♏	[illegible]	♉	[illegible]
♐	[illegible]	♊	[illegible]
♑	Capricorn [illegible]	♋	Cancer
♒	Aquarius [illegible]	♌	Leo
♓	Pisces [illegible]	♍	[illegible]

8 What if the Daily Moon is in my sign?

[illegible] two and a bit [illegible] The Moon takes a month to go around the chart through all the signs. If you're a Virgo [illegible] in Virgo, then when the Moon is in Virgo, we know that the Moon is going over the spot where the Sun was when you were born. Put the Sun and the Moon together in the same [illegible] same place and you get a New Moon. In this case it's a personal New Moon [illegible] and your personal Sun. It's a time of renewal [illegible] also be an emotional hot spot for you!

CHAPTER 11

Folklore Moons Through the Year

Over the past few years, as interest in the Moon (and, dare I say, Moonology) has increased across the world, so too has interest in the traditional folklore names for each Full Moon. These traditional names correspond to the calendar months or the seasons of the year, rather than to the astrological sign that each is in.

The idea of naming Moons dates back centuries and surely reflects the deep human instinct to measure time by nature rather than by clocks, which of course is what we used to do. Some names were recorded in Europe as early as the 16th century, when country life was ruled by the rhythm of planting, growing and harvesting.

When English settlers carried their traditions to the New World, the names mingled with those used by Native American peoples, who already had their own rich system of naming each Full Moon after seasonal signs in nature, from animal migrations to harvest times. Over the centuries, this blend of English, colonial and Indigenous naming formed the list we know today, before it was popularized in American farming almanacs.

These names aren't astrological, but they carry a gentle poetry that links us to an older, more earth-based way of seeing time.

Each one reflects what was happening in the natural world at that moment – the changes in weather, the crops in the ground or the behaviour of animals. They're a lovely reminder that the Moon doesn't just mark the months – She tells the story of the seasons.

Full Moon names in the northern hemisphere

◗ January: Moon after Yule, Wolf Moon, Fox Moon

This is the month when wolves (or foxes) howled through the cold midwinter nights, and yes, the first Full Moon after Christmas. In northern climates food was scarce, the ground was frozen and life depended on endurance and warmth.

The Wolf Moon invites stillness and reflection. It's a time to be wily like a fox as you plan out your year. Rebuild your strength and reconnect with your inner resources before the year begins to stir. Spiritually, it's a reminder that the coldest seasons will eventually pass.

◗ February: Snow Moon, Hunger Moon

The Snow Moon takes its name from February's heavy snowfalls across much of the northern hemisphere, while the Hunger Moon refers to the hard conditions that made hunting difficult. The world outside was quiet and blanketed in white, and supplies ran low.

This Moon symbolizes perseverance. It's a chance to slow down, conserve energy and focus on what truly matters. Under the Snow Moon, simplicity becomes sacred – warmth, nourishment and gratitude for life's small comforts.

◗ March: Worm Moon, Crow Moon

As the snow melts and the soil softens, the worms reappear and the crows start cawing again – early signs that spring is returning.

This is the turning point of the year, when the ground begins to breathe once more.

The Worm Moon brings energy for renewal. It's time to exhale and clear away the old to make room for the new, both physically and emotionally. The world awakens, and so do we.

◗ April: Pink Moon, Sprouting Grass Moon

The name Pink Moon comes from the wild ground phlox, a pink-flowering plant that blossoms in April across parts of North America. The name Sprouting Grass Moon also symbolizes spring, when new shoots rise and the earth comes alive with colour.

This is a warm and joyful name for the Moon of beginnings and creativity. It encourages growth, optimism and fresh ideas as the new astrological year begins. The Pink Moon invites us to plant seeds – real or symbolic – and trust that they'll take root.

◗ May: Flower Moon, Corn-Planting Moon

Flowers are at their peak in May, painting meadows and gardens everywhere. For early farmers, May was also the month for planting corn, an essential crop for the year ahead.

The Flower Moon represents abundance and fertility, both of the earth and the imagination. It's a time for manifestation and gratitude, not necessarily in that order. Whatever you nurture now, whether a dream, a garden or a relationship, can flourish under this Moon's light.

◗ June: Rose Moon, Flower Moon, Strawberry Moon

Strawberries ripen for harvesting now, while roses and flowers continue to bloom. This Moon's gentle warmth and long days bring a sense of fulfilment and sweetness.

The Strawberry Moon encourages enjoyment and gratitude. It's about celebrating the fruits of your labour and appreciating the beauty that surrounds you as we approach the mid-point of the year. The world is full of life and colour – be a part of it.

◗ July: Thunder Moon, Buck Moon

Frequent thunderstorms in New England gave this Moon Her name. It's also called the Buck Moon because this is when young male deer begin to grow their antlers.

This is a powerful Moon, like thunder and the deer, full of vitality and drive. It's ideal for bold action and determination. Thunder clears the air, and symbolically, this Moon encourages us to do the same, releasing tension and moving forwards with strength into the second half of the year.

◗ August: Sturgeon Moon

This Moon takes Her name from the sturgeon that were once most abundant at this time of year in the Great Lakes region. These large fish were a vital food source and a sign of nature's generosity.

The Sturgeon Moon represents perseverance. Like the sturgeon, maybe you need to swim against the current to achieve your goals. It's also about endurance – sturgeons can live for decades. Represented by one of the oldest species on Earth (sturgeon fossils date back over 200 million years), this Moon also carries the energy of resilience. Keep going!

◗ September: Harvest Moon

This Moon is so named because She falls near the autumnal equinox, when farmers worked late into the night to gather crops by Her bright light.

The Harvest Moon rises earlier than usual, stretching the twilight and extending the working day. She's a reminder that hard work can bring a good harvest. It may be time to reap what you've sown. Spiritually, this Moon invites rewards and closure. Celebrate your achievements and share your abundance with others.

◗ October: Hunter's Moon

Once the harvest was complete, it was time to hunt and prepare for winter. The light of the Hunter's Moon gave people time to stock up food for the cold months ahead.

This Moon symbolizes readiness and focus. It's perfect for tying up loose ends and setting practical goals. Spiritually, it's about preparation – knowing what to keep, what to release and how to sustain yourself through the darker season ahead. It's also about keeping your eyes on the prize, whatever you're chasing.

◗ November: Frosty Moon, Beaver Moon

November was the last month to set beaver traps before the waterways froze, and when the first heavy frosts arrived. Both names reflect a turning point, when the last of the year's warmer outdoor work was completed.

The Beaver Moon is associated with preparation and protection, and also about the power of hard work and cooperation (beavers work hard, and in teams). It's a good moment to secure your foundations – at home, at work and within yourself. The frost outside reminds us to appreciate the warmth within.

◗ December: Moon Before Yule, Cold Moon

This is the Moon before Christmas, when the temperature really begins to drop and the nights grow long. Moon Before Yule recalls the ancient midwinter festival marking the return of the Sun once we're through the winter solstice – the shortest day and longest night of the year. The Cold Moon brings closure and reflection.

It's a time to rest, to look back on the year and to prepare your heart for renewal. Even in the darkest nights, the Moon reminds us that light will return. Gather round in the warmth with people you love, for the Cold Moon is here, but then comes renewal.

Full Moon names in the southern hemisphere

While the previous Full Moon names follow the rhythm of the northern seasons, life south of the equator dances to a different rhythm. The Moons of Australia, Aotearoa (New Zealand) and the wider southern world tell another story – one of heat and dust, rain and renewal, gum leaves and seagulls' calls.

Long before European or modern interpretations, First Nations Australians, and Māori in Aotearoa, held – and still hold – intricate systems of lunar and seasonal knowledge, deeply connected to country, community and story.

The list that follows was inspired by ideas shared by others and shaped by my own observations of the living landscape I call home – a creative reflection of the southern cycle, honouring the seasons and the sky of this part of the world.

◗ January: Summer's Moon, Cicada Moon, Sea Breeze Moon

High summer. Along the coast, seagulls cry above white-tipped waves, while inland the air hums with cicadas hidden in the trees. Days are long and glow like a drop of white wine in the Sun; evenings soften into pink light. This Moon celebrates warmth, vitality and connection.

This is a time for gratitude and community – to enjoy the season's energy with those you love and to let yourself shine, like skin slicked with sun lotion. Savour the long, hot nights as much as the golden days, and remember how good it feels simply to be alive in the light.

◗ February: Hot Moon, Fire Moon, Lover's Moon

The peak of the heat. Under the Fire Moon, the air shimmers and the horizon wavers above sand baked by the Sun. In the high branches, koalas doze, their newborn joeys clinging tight, half-asleep in the haze. Across the land, bushfires flare and fade, clearing old growth and reminding us of nature's fierce renewal and of nature's dangers.

This Moon teaches balance and self-care. Move gently, drink water deeply and make space for stillness amid the intensity. Know that this is a powerful time of year – a test of endurance and grace. Keep your cool and tend to yourself with love. Bask in the Sun's warmth when you can, but don't burn.

◗ March: Cooling Moon, Harvest Moon South, Autumn Gold Moon

Heat lessens. Days are still bright, and the light feels gentler now – golden, slanted, almost nostalgic for summer's end. Grapes ripen on the vine, apples blush in the orchards and the countryside smells like golden hay bales.

The Cooling Moon signals the start of the southern harvest, when the year begins its slow descent towards rest. Slow your pace and enjoy the pause. Gather what's ready, release what's done and settle into a gentler rhythm before the inwards pull of autumn fully arrives.

◗ April: Rain Moon, Falling-Leaf Moon, Billabong Moon

Autumn rains return, billabongs fill and soil is nourished after months of beating Sun. Seeds germinate and the earth feels replenished.

The Rain Moon represents cleansing and renewal. Emotionally, it's an invitation to release what no longer serves and allow healing to flow. The symbolism here is all about releasing and letting go – even more than you did before. The falling leaves remind us that life goes in cycles and it's okay to move on, even in the fourth month of the year. The confusion from summer's heat clears.

◗ May: Fresh Moon, Mist Moon, Emu Moon

The air is crisp, mornings are misty and days bright. Trees renew their leaves and gardens thrive in cooler air. Overhead, the dark shape of the Emu in the Sky constellation stretches across the Milky Way – a celestial reminder that life, like our ancient lands, moves in cycles.

This Moon invites grounding and gratitude, a return to simplicity and quiet strength. It's a time to slow down, listen deeply and honour the wisdom of the earth beneath your feet and the sky above your head. As autumn edges towards winter, tie up loose ends and prepare to turn inwards. Enjoy the stillness and clarity – it's the calm before the year's next great turning.

◗ June: Middle Moon, Winter Hearth Moon, Southern Cross Moon

The midpoint of the year and the heart of winter. Fires burn steadily for those lucky enough to have them, nights stretch long and life slows. The Southern Cross gleams at its highest above the quiet Earth, a reminder that even in stillness, we're guided.

It's time to gather the clan for the middle of the year, and also spend time taking stock. The Middle Moon invites us into introspection and balance – a reminder that stillness has its own purpose. It's a time to gather your strength for what comes next.

◗ July: Snow Moon, Frost Moon South, Crystal Moon

In southern mountains, snow falls and the air turns crisp and clean. The Snow Moon stands for purity and quiet renewal. Rest deeply, nurture yourself and focus on inner warmth. It's the perfect Moon for gentle self-care and spiritual reset. Now is the time to take some time out if you possibly can. It's not about being frozen but gently suspended – a pause between the beginning and the end of the year. Use this stillness to dream and realign. What do you want to complete before the wheel turns again?

◗ August: Windy Moon, Wattle Moon, Change Moon

Late winter winds sweep through, scattering the old and clearing the way for spring. Wattle flowers bloom and, across Queensland, cane fields burn, their glow a reminder that sometimes renewal begins with release.

This Moon speaks of letting go – of clutter, habits and stories that no longer serve. Change stirs the air, unsettling yet cleansing. The wind rattles windows and hearts alike, blowing away the cobwebs we've learned to live with. Trust its wildness. Let it lift what's ready to move and carry you forwards into what comes next.

◗ September: Blessing Moon, Bloom Moon, Songbird Moon

Spring begins. Flowers bloom and daylight lengthens. The Blessing Moon celebrates renewal and growth. It's a joyful moment to welcome abundance and appreciate the beauty of the natural world returning to life. Paddocks turn green again after winter rain. Kookaburras laugh from gum trees, greeting the lengthening days, newborn lambs and calves graze and orchards hum with bees. Magpies carol from fence posts, honeyeaters flit amongst wattles and butterflies dance through the warming air.

This Moon is a time to live life as though it's alive, generous and full of promise – because it is!

◗ October: Roo Moon, Wildflower Moon, Jacaranda Moon

The light shifts again as daylight saving begins in many parts of the southern hemisphere, stretching the evenings and filling them with summery promises. The land is warming up. Kangaroos bound across open fields, wildflowers blaze in the outback and city streets turn lavender beneath the blooming jacaranda.

This is a time to move, leap into action and trust that the energy rising in you mirrors the world awakening around you.

◗ November: Quickening Moon, Humid Moon, Frangipani Moon

The pace quickens as summer draws near. Warm winds sweep across paddocks of ripening wheat, barley and oats, and the air hums with anticipation and humidity. Jacarandas make way for flame trees and frangipanis – summer is in the air.

This Moon the spirit of momentum. It's time to finish what you've started, to work with focus and drive while energy is high. Soon the days will stretch and celebrations will call you to rest and play – but for now, harness the warmth, the storms and the rising tempo of life. Breathe in vitality. The Quickening Moon reminds you that effort now leads to freedom later.

◗ December: End-of-Year Moon, Celebration Moon, Mango Moon

It's the height of summer Down Under. Days stretch long and golden, and the air thrums with cicadas and the sounds of barbecues in backyards. Heat shimmers through the gum leaves. Evenings invite laughter and late walks. The smell of salt, sunscreen and mangoes is in the air.

This Moon carries the spirit of celebration and completion. It's a time to gather with loved ones, breathe out and reflect on the year gone by, and to open your heart to joy. This End-of-Year Moon reminds us to pause, appreciate and simply live – bright, bold and fully present in the light.

Whether you live north or south of the equator, following the Full Moon names connects you to the rhythm of the natural world. These old and new names are simple markers of the seasons – reminders that time is circular, not linear.

Every month, the Full Moon rises as it always has, ancient and familiar, inviting us to pause and look up.

CHAPTER 12

Sacred Moon Rituals

Creating ritual is one of the oldest human instincts – as ancient as painting on cave walls or telling stories around a fire. A ritual is simply a meaningful act, done with intention. It gives rhythm to life, helps us mark turning points and connects us to something greater than ourselves – whether you call that Source, Spirit, the Divine or the Universe.

Since time immemorial, people have used rituals to honour the cycles of life and nature. Evidence from ancient burials shows that even our earliest ancestors marked life's transitions with care and beauty – perhaps by placing flowers with their loved ones. Across cultures and centuries, rituals have offered reassurance and renewal, aligning us with the rhythms of Mother Nature. People have gathered to honour the Moon's phases, the changing seasons, sunrise and sunset, the tides and the cycles of planting and harvest.

In India, *puja* ceremonies invite Divine energy through offerings of light, water, flowers and sound. In the Celtic world, fire festivals such as Beltane and Samhain celebrate the eternal dance of life, death and rebirth. Indigenous traditions use smoke and water ceremonies to honour the land and their ancestors. Though these rituals may look different, they all arise from the same longing – to feel connected: to the Earth, to our communities and to the unseen realms of Spirit.

Many ancient calendars – from Babylonian to Celtic – followed lunar or lunisolar patterns, showing how deeply the Moon once guided daily and spiritual life. Today's Moon rituals, like those I've set out in this book, continue that ancient tradition. When we light a candle and write our intentions at the New Moon, or reflect on what we're ready to release at the Full Moon, we're doing what our ancestors did – turning to nature as our teacher, mirror and guide.

Modern psychology now confirms what mystics have always known: rituals are powerful. They help us slow down, shift our awareness and focus on what truly matters. In my experience, they're also incredible tools for creating change and aligning with the life we most want to live.

Rituals are where the spiritual and the everyday meet. They bring a touch of the sacred into our ordinary lives and help us anchor celestial energies in a real, tangible way. The practices in this chapter will show you how to work with the elements and honour the Moon's cycles – just as countless generations have done before you.

Simple rituals for each element

The elements of Fire, Earth, Air and Water are more than astrological symbols – they're the building blocks of life itself. Found in nearly every spiritual and healing tradition, from indigenous medicine wheels to Greek philosophy, Ayurveda, Taoism and Wicca, they remind us of our connection to the natural world and to our own inner balance.

Working consciously with the elements allows us to draw on their gifts: Fire for inspiration and courage; Earth for grounding and stability; Air for clarity and communication and Water for emotion and flow. Just remember that we don't do rituals for the Divine. God/dess doesn't need our rituals! We do them for ourselves, to ground the energies.

Drawing on these traditions, I began to include rituals in my own teachings as a way to bring the energies from the heavens to your home! Rituals are sacred gateways between the physical and spiritual worlds. When we work with them through the Moon's cycle, we bring magic down to Earth.

You can use rituals at any stage of the lunar cycle. I use them at the New Moon to set intentions, at the Full Moon for release and in the spaces between for integration and reflection. Each one helps you connect to the rhythm of nature and your own energy.

Before you begin, roll out your yoga mat or lay down a towel, light some oil in your burner and put on some beautiful music. I love Edo and Jo, Solfeggio Frequencies, and Deva Premal, among others (*see page 249*). Take a few minutes for a meditation or a simple 4-6-8 breathing exercise (inhale for 4, hold for 6, exhale for 8). When you finish your ritual, pull an oracle card about whatever is on your mind and journal about what it brings up.

Fire: ignite, act, transform

- Element of: Aries, Leo, Sagittarius
- Keywords: passion, energy, courage, transformation
- Tools: candle, matches, journal, pen, music, fireproof bowl

Fire is the spark that turns intention into action. It burns away fear and fuels creation, reminding you that light always follows the darkness.

New Moon Fire ritual to ignite your intention

Light a white or beeswax candle. Say:

'As I light this fire, I awaken my purpose
and welcome new beginnings.'

Visualize your new intentions glowing in the flame, sending their light out into the Universe.

First Quarter Moon Fire ritual to take aligned action

Light a candle and, as it burns, commit to one bold step. Then say:

'I feed this flame with action and courage.
I move forwards with confidence.'

Do one tangible thing that propels your dream ahead.

Full Moon Fire ritual to burn and release

Write down what you're ready to let go of: fears, frustrations or habits that dim your light.

Safely burn the paper, saying:

'As this burns, I am set free. My energy is renewed.'

Last Quarter Moon Fire ritual to reflect and refine

Gaze at the flicker of a candle. Ask yourself what you've learned since the Full Moon. Say:

'As this flame softens, I release what no
longer serves and keep the wisdom.'

Dark Moon Fire ritual to ignite your inner spark

Sit quietly in darkness. Visualize a tiny golden flame within your heart. Whisper:

'Even in darkness, my light remains.'

Daily Moon Fire ritual for a quick energy reset

Light a candle and take three deep breaths. Feel your inner fire awaken.

~

Earth: ground, grow, manifest

- Element of: Taurus, Virgo, Capricorn
- Keywords: grounding, abundance, stability, patience
- Tools: crystals, soil, plants, herbs, journal, a pen

Earth is the element of manifestation. It helps you anchor your dreams and bring spiritual ideas into form. It reminds you to trust Divine timing and move steadily forwards.

Earth Rituals

New Moon Earth ritual to plant your intentions

Hold a crystal or press your palm to the earth. Say:

'I plant my dreams in fertile soil.
They grow strong and steady.'

Write down your wishes and bury the paper or place it under a plant pot.

First Quarter Moon Earth ritual to take root

Spend time outdoors or ground your feet on the floor. Say:

'I am grounded and guided.
I take practical steps towards my goals.'

Full Moon Earth ritual for gratitude and growth

Gather natural items such as leaves, herbs, flowers or stones and place them on your altar. Say:

'I honour all that has blossomed.
I am grateful for abundance.'

Think about three things that have flourished since the last New Moon.

Last Quarter Moon Earth ritual for clearing

Declutter your space or tidy your altar. Say:

'I release the old to make space for the new.'

Physically clear something from your environment and let go to grow.

Dark Moon Earth ritual to rest and restore

Lie down and visualize roots anchoring you deep in the soil. Whisper:

'I return to the earth to be renewed.'

Daily Moon Earth ritual for morning grounding

Before your day begins, place your hand over your heart and say:

'I am safe and supported in my body.'

~

Air: clarity, thought, communication

- Element of: Gemini, Libra, Aquarius
- Keywords: insight, ideas, voice, movement
- Tools: incense, feathers, music, journal, a pen, breath

Air is the element of the mind and the messenger of Spirit. It governs your thoughts, words and how you share your truth. Working with Air invites clarity and inspiration.

Air Rituals

New Moon Air ritual to speak your intentions

Light incense or hold a feather. Say:

'My words are spells. My voice creates my world.'

Write your intentions and read them out loud with conviction.

First Quarter Moon Air ritual to move ideas into motion

Take a few deep, conscious breaths. Say:

'I breathe life into my ideas and allow inspiration to flow.'

Then take one practical step that turns thought into form.

Full Moon Air ritual to clear the mind

Cleanse your space with sage or incense. Say:

'I release mental clutter and breathe in clarity.'

Write down any thoughts, worries or stories that feel heavy. Safely burn or tear the paper to release them.

Last Quarter Moon Air ritual to reflect and reframe

Write a list of insights from this Moon cycle. Say:

'I honour my lessons and transform them into wisdom.'

You can speak your gratitude aloud to seal the learning.

Dark Moon Air ritual to still the winds

Sit quietly in meditation and focus on your breath. Whisper:

'I am the calm beneath the changing skies.'

Daily Moon Air ritual for morning breathwork

Start the day with three rounds of 4-6-8 breathing (inhale for 4, hold for 6, exhale for 8). Let your thoughts settle.

~

Water: emotion, intuition, healing

- Element of: Cancer, Scorpio, Pisces
- Keywords: emotion, intuition, reflection, compassion
- Tools: bowl of water, sea salt, rose petals

Water cleanses, heals and restores flow. It teaches us to trust our emotions and surrender to the tides of life.

☾ Water Rituals

New Moon Water ritual to flow into intention

Fill a bowl with clean or blessed water. Say:

'I infuse this water with my dreams.
My desires flow with grace.'

Dip your fingers in and sprinkle the water on your altar or yourself.

First Quarter Moon Water ritual to nurture the flow

Drink a glass of water mindfully. Say:

'As this water nourishes me, my dreams take shape.'

Visualize energy flowing freely through your life.

Full Moon Water ritual to cleanse and release

Take a ritual bath or shower with sea salt and rose petals. Say:

'I release the past and wash away
what no longer serves me.'

Imagine the water carrying your emotions into peace.

Last Quarter Moon Water ritual for emotional clarity

Sit with a bowl of water and gaze into its surface. Say:

'I see clearly what I feel. I honour my truth.'

Journal any insights that arise.

Dark Moon Water ritual for deep healing

Place a glass of water under the night sky. Whisper:

'In this stillness, I surrender. I am renewed.'

Drink it in the morning as a symbol of rebirth.

Daily Moon Water ritual to bless your drink

Each time you pour water, pause and say:

'This water carries light, love and healing.'

~

Working with the four elements keeps you connected to the natural world and to your own inner balance. Each time you honour them, you honour the sacred cycles of the Moon and the light and life within yourself.

Aligning your rituals with Moon signs

As you know, each New and Full Moon takes place in a different star sign each month, highlighting a specific area of your life. You can use the elemental rituals in this chapter alongside these sign-based focuses to personalize your practice.

New Moon ritual focus by star sign		
♈	Aries	The courage to live your dreams
♉	Taurus	Money manifesting
♊	Gemini	Better communications
♋	Cancer	Happier home life
♌	Leo	The confidence to strut your stuff
♍	Virgo	Increased organization
♎	Libra	Better love life
♏	Scorpio	Better sex life
♐	Sagittarius	Wishes around study and adventure
♑	Capricorn	Career ambitions
♒	Aquarius	Wishes for friends and the world
♓	Pisces	Increased connection to the Divine

Full Moon ritual focus by star sign		
♈	Aries	Find a balance between give and take
♉	Taurus	Think about your money matters
♊	Gemini	Slow down and be real with people
♋	Cancer	Feel more sure of yourself

♌	Leo	Consider what your friends need versus what you need
♍	Virgo	Remember the importance of being helpful
♎	Libra	See the beauty in life
♏	Scorpio	Bring passion back to your life
♐	Sagittarius	Keep life adventurous, not stagnant
♑	Capricorn	Release the need to control
♒	Aquarius	Detach and let go
♓	Pisces	Find peace amid duties and demands

Once you've worked with each element on its own, you may feel called to bring them together in a single ritual. This creates a complete energetic circuit, balancing passion (Fire), stability (Earth), clarity (Air) and flow (Water). When you unite the elements, you align with the wholeness of nature herself.

☾ Bringing It All Together

To begin, create your sacred space as you've learned. Roll out your mat or towel, light some oil in the burner, play gentle music and breathe deeply. Then gather one object to represent each of the elements:

- Fire: a candle or small flame
- Earth: a crystal, flower or pinch of soil
- Air: incense, a feather or a piece of paper and a pen
- Water: a small bowl of water or a seashell

Set your intention for the ritual. Take a moment with each element in turn, saying a simple prayer or affirmation.

Fire: *'I call on the energy of Fire to ignite my purpose and renew my passion.'*

Earth: *'I call on the energy of Earth to ground and sustain me.'*

Air: *'I call on the energy of Air to clear my mind and lift my thoughts.'*

Water: *'I call on the energy of Water to cleanse my heart and restore my flow.'*

When you're done, sit quietly and feel the balance within you: steady, alive, clear and open. If you wish, finish by taking an oracle card to guide your next step, then journal what you experienced.

~

I hope these rituals help you to realign or recharge whenever you feel the need. The more you honour the rhythm of the Moon, the more life itself begins to feel like a sacred ceremony.

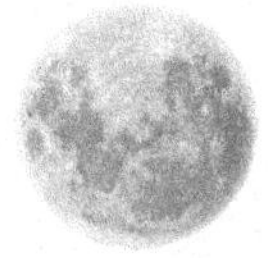

Conclusion

So there you have it – pretty much everything you need to know about the Moon in order to become a Moonologer. Now you understand what that amazing-looking thing up in the skies is there for! Or is it? Who really knows?

The Moon has always been mysterious. However, if you take the time to work with the lunar cycles, one thing is certain – *your life will change*. As I said at the start of this book, I've seen it in my own life and I've had it reported back to me by countless readers over the years.

So the main idea of working with the Moon is to get really clear about what you want and to write that down, or say it out loud, or doodle/draw it at the time of the New Moon. And then to use the Full Moon as a time to empty yourself of any upsets and to refill yourself with gratitude for all the good in your life.

Also, take a moment every month to check which sign the New or Full Moon is in, and then refer to the guides in this book to see how that's best used. And notice, too, which House the New or Full Moon is in your chart.

If and when you have something important coming up, check where the Moon is or will be. If you work with the Moon, life will flow more smoothly. So, get in tune with the Moon!

Conclusion

S[illegible] pretty much everything you need [illegible] [illegible] [illegible] [illegible]

The Moon [illegible] [illegible] with the [illegible] cycles [illegible] the [illegible] [illegible] of this book. [illegible] it is my [illegible] and I wished [illegible] [illegible] over the years.

So the main [illegible] working with the Moon is to really [illegible] about what you want and to write that down [illegible] it out [illegible] at the starting of the New Moon. And then [illegible] use the [illegible] [illegible]

[illegible] every month to check which sign the New or Full Moon is [illegible] to the [illegible] in this book [illegible] which [illegible] the New or Full Moon [illegible] in your chart.

If and when you have anything important coming up, check where the Moon is or will be. If you [illegible] with the Moon, life will flow more smoothly [illegible] with the Moon [illegible]

APPENDIX A

Quick Reference Guide to the Signs and Houses

The 12 signs and what they represent

In case you're not already familiar with the main themes and qualities of each zodiac sign, here's a basic list. The New Moon (and also the Daily, Full and Quarter Moon) in the 12 zodiac signs will trigger the following themes:

♈	**Aries**	Beginnings, bravery, boldness, spontaneity
♉	**Taurus**	Sensuality, earthiness, practicality
♊	**Gemini**	Communications, travel, neighbours, siblings
♋	**Cancer**	Home and family, domestic life, privacy
♌	**Leo**	Fun, creativity, kids (your own or someone else's), flirtation
♍	**Virgo**	Service to others, duties, daily working life, wellbeing, small animals
♎	**Libra**	You, significant others, lovers, VIPs, foes, balance, harmony, marriage, relationships

(continued)

♏	**Scorpio**	Sex, death, anything taboo, jealousy, rebirth, taxes, other people's money
♐	**Sagittarius**	Travel, study, freedom, the Great Cosmic Quest, religion, higher education
♑	**Capricorn**	Work, ambition, career; where you leave your mark
♒	**Aquarius**	Friends, social networks, groups, The Thing Wished For, hopes and dreams
♓	**Pisces**	The deepest, darkest and most delicate part of your psyche; spirituality, fears, institutions

The 12 Houses and what they represent

Below is a list of the keywords for each of the 12 Houses – each House covers one part of life or another.

1st House	This rules the way you come across to others, your image and the way others see you.
2nd House	This rules property and possessions. It's also about your values and self-worth.
3rd House	This is where you keep your communications skills. It's also about short trips, siblings and neighbours.
4th House	This part of your chart is about home and family and all that entails – your private life.
5th House	This part of your chart relates to sexy romance, creativity and children (your own and other people's).
6th House	This rules body and mind, wellbeing, your daily work and health routines.
7th House	This is about marriage, your beloved, your ex, people you consider enemies, commitment and VIPs.

(continued)

8th House	This is about anything 'taboo', such as sex, death and taxes. Also, other people's money and joint financial ventures.
9th House	This is where you see the big picture, expand your horizons, study, travel. And the Great Cosmic Quest.
10th House	This rules ambitions, career and life goals. What you're 'known' for – your professional life.
11th House	This is the House of Hopes and Wishes; it rules friends, connections and social circles.
12th House	This is the deepest and most sensitive part of your chart; it relates to fears and spirituality: what's hidden.

If you'd like a really helpful visual representation of the Houses, please visit moonologybook.com/Houses.

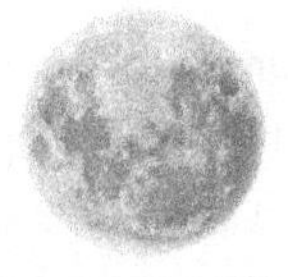

APPENDIX B

The Lunar Nodes

The lunar nodes are the points where the orbit of the Moon crosses the ecliptic – an imaginary line on the sky that marks the annual path of the Sun. They're wonderful to use as a predictor. Whichever House the north node is in, is where you'll find happiness and fulfilment, and whichever House the south node is in, is where you may well feel drawn, or even somehow compelled, to stay – but you need to work on yourself to move away from the south node House and towards the north node House. You do that by observing your own patterns of behaviour. When you have …

◗ North node in the 1st House/south node in the 7th

You may be obsessed with the idea of having a relationship, but standing on your own two feet will make you happier.

◗ North node in the 2nd House/south node in the 8th

All sorts of deep and dark subjects and taboo activities might be tempting you, but getting real and sorting out your finances will make you happier.

◗ North node in the 3rd House/south node in the 9th

You may enjoy the sound of your own voice and waffling, but you'll find happiness through real communication with others.

◗ North node in the 4th House/south node in the 10th

Your career may be seducing you and making you feel it's the most important thing in the world but home and family is what will bring you happiness.

◗ North node in the 5th House/south node in the 11th

You may be obsessed with your friends and the idea of freedom, but what will make you happy now is creative expression.

◗ North node in the 6th House/south node in the 12th

The thought of running away from your life might be an enjoyable daydream, but knuckling down and doing what you have to is what will actually fulfil you now.

◗ North node in the 7th House/south node in the 1st

You stand to gain a lot from being in a relationship now. Yes, your buttons might get pushed but think of the opportunities for character growth.

◗ North node in the 8th House/south node in the 2nd

While you may feel compelled to worry about your finances now, like a proper grown-up, good old-fashioned hot sex is what you need right now.

◗ North node in the 9th House/south node in the 3rd

Lots of light-hearted chatter and meaningless small talk might feel like an easy option but it's the truth that will set you free.

◗ North node in the 10th House/south node in the 4th

Family first is a wonderful motto to live by, except for now, when you have cosmic encouragement to throw yourself into your career if you want fulfilment.

◗ North node in the 11th House/south node in the 5th

You know that person you're so obsessed with and want to make your lover? He or she would likely be better off as your friend.

◗ North node in the 12th House/south node in the 6th

Trying to keep your life working like clockwork may seem vital but what really matters is inner peace.

Lunar nodes 2026–2035

What follows is for UK time: there may be one-day variations in other parts of the world.

Date	Lunar node
27 July 2026	The north node moves into Aquarius and the south node moves into Leo.
26 March 2028	The north node moves into Capricorn and the south node moves into Cancer.
23 September 2029	The north node moves into Sagittarius and the south node moves into Gemini.
20 March 2031	The north node moves into Scorpio and the south node moves into Taurus.
2 December 2032	The north node moves into Libra and the south node moves into Aries.
3 June 2034	The north node moves into Virgo and the south node moves into Pisces.
30 November 2035	The north node moves into Leo and the south node moves into Aquarius.

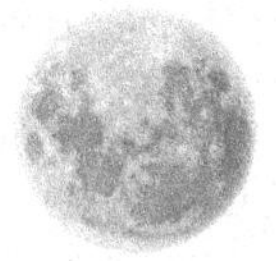

Bibliography

Banzhaf, Hajo and Haebler, Anna, *Key Words for Astrology* (Weiser Books, 1996)

Boehrer, K.T., *Declination: The Other Dimension* (Fortunate Press, 1994)

Cooper, Diana, *A Little Light on the Spiritual Laws* (Findhorn Press, 2007)

Cunningham, Donna, *Moon Signs: The Key to Your Inner Life* (Ballantine Books, 1993)

Graham, L., *The Ascended Masters* (AuthorHouse, 2005)

Hoffman, Jennifer, *Ascending Into Miracles* (Feed your Muse Press, 2011)

Mason, Sophia, *Forecasting with the New, Full and Quarter Moons* (American Federation of Astrologers, 2013)

Melchizedek, Drunvalo, *The Ancient Secret of the Flower of Life: v.1* (Light Technology, 1999)

Milanovich, Dr Norma J. and McCune, Dr Shirley, *The Light Shall Set You Free* (Athena Publishing, 1996)

Myss, Caroline, *Anatomy Of The Spirit* (Bantam, 1997)

Purna, Svami, *The Truth Will Set You Free* (New Age Books, 2008)

Rogers-Gallagher, Kim, *Astrology For The Light Side of the Future* (ACS Publications Inc., 1998)

Rudhyar, Dane, *The Lunation Cycle* (Aurora Press, 1986)

Spiller, Jan, *New Moon Astrology* (Bantam, 2001)

Sri Sakthi Amma, *Connect with the Divine* (Om Sakti Narayani Siddar Pedam Charitable Trust, 2011)

Virtue, Doreen and Boland Yasmin, *Archangel Astrology 101* (Hay House, 2014)

Virtue, Doreen, *Archangels And Ascended Masters* (Hay House, 2004)

Virtue, Doreen, *Divine Magic: The Seven Sacred Secrets of Manifestation* (Hay House, 2015)

Worwood, Valerie Ann, *The Fragrant Mind* (Bantam, 1997)

Yogananda, Paramahamsa, *Autobiography of a Yogi* (Yogoda Satsanga Society of India, 2013)

Resources

Music

Below is a short list of music I highly recommended for spiritual seekers. Download it and listen while you're doing your New Moon manifesting or Full Moon forgiveness and gratitude ceremonies – or any time at all!

Kirtan Alive! Edo and Jo – edoandjo.com/shop

Mark Watson – marklwatsonmusic.com

Deva Premal and Miten – devapremalmiten.com

Nirinjan Kaur – facebook.com/nirinjankaur

Mirabai Ceiba – mirabaiceiba.com

Websites

yasminboland.com
Visit my site to find out which sign the Moon is in, the date of the next New Moon, a Daily Moon Message and much more.

www.timeanddate.com/moon/phases
A wonderful resource for finding out about New, Quarter and Full Moon times and dates.

Permissions

The Full Moon Forgiveness and Karma Release Formula on page 145 was inspired by the work of Catherine Ponder and the late Charles Fillmore, and reprinted with the kind permission of Catherine Ponder.

A special thank you to Doreen Virtue for her kind permission to use material from the book we co-authored, *Angel Astrology 101* (Hay House, 2014).

About the Author

Award-winning astrologer and *Sunday Times* best-selling author Yasmin Boland was born in Germany to English/Irish/Maltese parents and grew up in Hobart, Tasmania. After university, she worked as a journalist, which led her to 'mainland' Australia and eventually to London, where she worked as a journalist and radio and TV producer.

In the 1990s, learning how to meditate completely changed Yasmin's life and opened her up to astrology. Her passion for astrology eventually became her profession, and Yasmin is now one of the most widely read astrology writers on the planet. Yasmin loves all astrology but has a special interest in the Moon.

Yasmin has been named as one of the '100 Most Spiritually Influential Living People.' She's the bestselling author of *Moonology*™, *Astrology Made Easy*, *The Mercury Retrograde Book*, Moonology™ *Oracle Cards* and *Moonology*™ *Manifestation Oracle Cards*, *Moonology*™ *Messages Oracle* and *The Dark Moon Oracle*.

We hope you enjoyed this Hay House book. If you'd like to receive our online catalog featuring additional information on Hay House books and products, or if you'd like to find out more about the Hay Foundation, please contact:

HAY HOUSE AUSTRALIA PUBLISHING PTY LTD
18/36 Ralph St., Alexandria NSW 2015
Phone: +61 2 9669 4299
www.hayhouse.com.au

Published in the United States of America by:
HAY HOUSE LLC,
P.O. Box 5100, Carlsbad, CA 92018-5100
(760) 431-7695 or (800) 654-5126
www.hayhouse.com® • www.hayfoundation.org

Published in the United Kingdom by:
HAY HOUSE UK LTD
1st Floor Crawford Corner,
91–93 Baker Street, London W1U 6QQ
www.hayhouse.co.uk

Published in India by:
HAY HOUSE PUBLISHERS (INDIA) PVT LTD
Muskaan Complex, Plot No. 3,
B-2, Vasant Kunj, New Delhi 110 070
Phone: +91 11 41761620
www.hayhouse.co.in